GROSS
GUIDES
To Psychology
OCR AS

RICHARD GROSS
SARAH BYRNE

HODDER
EDUCATION
AN HACHETTE UK COMPANY

Picture credits

The authors and publishers would like to thank the following for the use of the photographs in this volume:

Figure 1.1 © Moritz Wussow – Fotolia; Figure 2.4 © Marek Kosmal – Fotolia; Figure 3.4 © Autism Research Centre, Department of Psychiatry, University of Cambridge; Figure 3.5 © Great Ape Trust; Figure 3.6 © Great Ape Trust; Figure 4.3 © ALBERT BANDURA, STANFORD CENTER ON ADOLESCENCE, STANFORD UNIVERSITY; Figure 4.5 © Christine Stuermer – Fotolia; Figure 5.2 © DPA/Press Association Images; Figure 6.2 From the film Obedience © 1968 by Stanley Milgram, © renewed 1993 by Alexandra Milgram; Figure 6.3 © BBC; Figure 6.5 © AP/Press Association Images; Figure 7.2 © 20th Century Fox / The Kobal Collection; Figure 7.3 © kentoh – Fotolia; Figure 7.4 © Sean Gladwell – Fotolia; Figure 8.1 © Underwood & Underwood/Corbis; Figure 9.1 © Universal History Archive/Getty Images. Image of open book used throughout © blackred/iStockphoto.

We would also like to thank the following:

Figure 6.6 reproduced from *Journal of Personality and Social Psychology*, vol. 13, no. 4, Piliavin, I., Rodin, J., and Piliavin, J., 'Good Samaritanism: an underground phenomenon?', pp. 289–99, 1969, with permission from Elsevier.

Tables 3.1 and 3.3 reprinted from *Journal of Verbal Learning and Verbal Behavior*, vol. 13, Loftus, E. and Palmer, J., 'Reconstruction of automobile destruction: An example of the interaction between language and memory', pp. 585–589, 1974, with permission from Elsevier.

Every effort has been made to trace and acknowledge ownership of copyright. The publishers will be glad to make suitable arrangements with any copyright holders whom it has not been possible to contact.

Orders: please contact Bookpoint Ltd, 130 Milton Park, Abingdon, Oxon OX14 4SB. Telephone: (44) 01235 827720. Fax: (44) 01235 400454. Lines are open from 9.00 - 5.00, Monday to Saturday, with a 24 hour message answering service. You can also order through our website www.hoddereducation.co.uk

If you have any comments to make about this, or any of our other titles, please send them to educationenquiries@hodder.co.uk

British Library Cataloguing in Publication Data
A catalogue record for this title is available from the British Library

ISBN: 9781444168082

Published 2012
Impression number   10 9 8 7 6 5 4 3 2 1
Year   2016, 2015, 2014, 2013, 2012

Hachette UK's policy is to use papers that are natural, renewable and recyclable products and made from wood grown in sustainable forests. The logging and manufacturing processes are expected to conform to the environmental regulations of the country of origin.

Illustrations by Barking Dog Art and DC Graphic Design Limited, Swanley Village, Kent
Typeset by DC Graphic Design Limited, Swanley Village, Kent.

Printed in Italy for Hodder Education, An Hachette UK Company, 338 Euston Road, London NW1 3BH by L.E.G.O

Contents

How to use this book

This book will help you revise for your AS exams in the OCR Psychology specification. It is designed so that you can use it alongside any appropriate textbook, including Richard Gross's *Psychology: The Science of Mind and Behaviour* and we have included page references to this book where appropriate. —————————

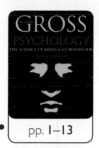

pp. 1–13

Each of the 15 Core Studies are covered, with the headline facts and knowledge you will need for each, accompanied by evaluation material and questions to help test your understanding.

Perspectives and psychological investigations are also covered in a colourful and exciting way, to help you retain and recall the information.

Sarah Byrne is an examiner for a leading awarding body and at the beginning of the book you will find her guidance on how to approach the exam structure.

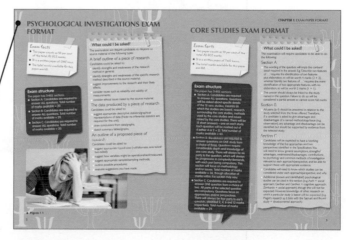

PSYCHOLOGICAL INVESTIGATIONS EXAM FORMAT

Exam facts

- This paper counts as 30 per cent of the total AS GCE marks.
- It is a written paper of ONE hour.
- The total marks available for this paper are 60.

Exam structure

The paper has THREE sections:
- Section A: Candidates are required to answer ALL questions. Total number of marks available = 20.
- Section B: Candidates are required to answer ALL questions. Total number of marks available = 20.
- Section C: Candidates are required to answer ALL questions. Total number of marks available = 20.

What could I be asked?

The examination will require candidates to respond to source material of the following types:

A brief outline of a piece of research

Candidates could be asked to:
- identify strengths and weaknesses of the research method in general;
- identify strengths and weaknesses of the specific research method described in the source material;
- suggest improvements to the research and their likely effects;
- consider issues such as reliability and validity of measurements;
- consider ethical issues raised by the source material.

The data produced by a piece of research

Candidates could be asked to:
- suggest appropriate descriptive statistics/graphical representations of data (Note: no inferential statistics are required for this unit);
- draw conclusions from data/graphs;
- sketch summary tables/graphs.

An outline of a proposed piece of research

Candidates could be asked to:
- suggest appropriate hypotheses (null/alternate, one-tailed/two-tailed);
- suggest how variables might be operationalised/measured;
- suggest appropriate samples/sampling methods;
- outline possible procedures;
- evaluate suggestions you have made.

▲ Figure 1.1

CORE STUDIES EXAM FORMAT

Exam facts

- This paper counts as 70 per cent of the total AS GCE marks.
- It is a written paper of TWO hours.
- The total marks available for this paper are 120.

Exam structure

The paper has THREE sections:

- Section A: Candidates are required to answer ALL questions. Questions will be asked about specific details of the 15 core studies, theories on which the studies are based, research surrounding the core studies, methods used by the core studies and issues raised by the core studies. There will be 15 short answers – one on each study. Each question will be marked out of 4 (either 4 or 2 + 2). Total number of marks available = 60.

- Section B: Candidates are required to answer questions on ONE study from a choice of three. Questions require considerable depth and knowledge of one core study. There will always be six parts to the question, which will always be progressive in complexity/demands, with each part being compulsory. This section will focus on methodology and/or issues. Total number of marks available = 36, though allocation of marks within the section may vary.

- Section C: Candidates are required to answer ONE question from a choice of two. All parts of the selected question are compulsory. Questions focus on approaches and/or perspectives. There will always be four parts to each question, awarded 2, 4, 6 and 12 marks respectively. Total number of marks available = 24.

What could I be asked?

The examination will require candidates to be able to do the following:

Section A

- The wording of the question will imply the content/detail required in the answer. E.g. 'Describe *two* features of …' requires the identification of *two* features plus elaboration, so will be worth 4 marks (2 + 2), whereas 'Identify *two* features of …' requires the mere identification of two appropriate features, with no elaboration, so will be worth 2 marks (1 + 1).

- The answer should always be linked to the study named in the question. Failure to do so will be considered a partial answer, so cannot score full marks.

Section B

- All parts (a–f) should be answered in relation to the study selected from the three offered. Therefore, if a candidate is asked to give advantages and disadvantages of a named methodology/issue (e.g. observation), any advantage and disadvantage can be identified, but should be supported by evidence from the selected study.

Section C

- Candidates will be expected to have a 'working knowledge' of the five approaches and two perspectives identified in the Specification. You will need to know general assumptions, strengths/advantages, weaknesses/disadvantages, contributions to psychology and common methods of investigation relevant to each approach/perspective, and be able to support these with appropriate evidence.

- Candidates will need to know which studies can be considered under each approach/perspective, and why.

- Additional (known and identifiable!) psychological studies can be cited in this section (e.g. Asch + social approach; Gardner and Gardner + cognitive approach; Zimbardo + social approach), though this will not be expected. However, knowledge of other research on which a particular study is based will be expected (e.g. Piaget's research as it links with the Samuel and Bryant study + developmental approach).

THE FOUR INVESTIGATIVE TECHNIQUES

Self-reports

This method involves some form of questioning (interview, questionnaire, survey), in which the participant rather than the test administrator (researcher) selects and reports/records the response(s).

Interviews involve some form of direct verbal questioning of the participant by the researcher, though they can differ in how structured the questions are. The four main types of interview are: structured, semi-structured, clinical and unstructured.

Questionnaires are written methods of gaining data from participants. The researcher does not necessarily have to be present, as the participant answers questions by writing on a pre-formatted question paper.

Surveys are also written methods of gaining data. However, the researcher asks the participant a direct verbal question and then records the response in written format, usually on a pre-prepared 'coding' chart.

Strengths of self-reports

✔ Generally, surveys and questionnaires collect large amounts of standardised data relatively quickly and conveniently, making results more representative of the target population/population as a whole.

✔ Questionnaires and surveys are highly replicable, so similarities/differences and trends in behaviour can be identified.

Weaknesses of self-reports

✘ Generally, questionnaires and surveys lack flexibility, particularly if closed questions are asked, not allowing participants to qualify or expand on their responses.

✘ Responses are open to being influenced by social desirability, where a participant responds with an answer they know is morally/socially acceptable, which may not be their own thoughts or feelings. Results are therefore invalid.

Strengths of experiments

Laboratory experiments:

✔ Highly controlled, so the effect of confounding variables (anything that could influence the DV) is minimised.

✔ Easily replicable.

✔ Can show cause and effect.

Field experiments:

✔ High in ecological validity.

✔ Demand characteristics can be avoided if participants do not know they are in a study.

Experiments

Experiments involve the study of 'cause and effect', so one variable (the independent variable/IV) is altered/manipulated to see what effect it has on another variable (the dependent variable/DV). The dependent variable is the variable that is measured, and the independent variable is the variable that is predicted to affect the dependent variable.

Other variables that could potentially influence the dependent variable, known as extraneous variables, should, whenever possible, be eliminated or controlled. Experiments are therefore frequently conducted in artificial environments, so the researcher can control potential extraneous variables to prevent them becoming confounding variables (variables that actually affect the dependent variable strongly enough to influence the results). Such experiments are known as laboratory experiments. Experiments can also be conducted in natural environments; these are known as field experiments. Obviously if a field experiment is used, the researcher has less control over extraneous variables.

Weaknesses of experiments

Laboratory experiments:

✘ Low in ecological validity.

✘ Often prone to demand characteristics.

✘ Ethical issues: deception often used, so informed consent is not obtained.

Field experiments:

✘ Low control over variables.

✘ Difficult to replicate.

✘ Difficult to record data.

✘ Ethical problems of consent, deception, invasion of privacy, etc.

Observations

Observations involve the precise measurement of naturally occurring behaviour, the aim being to observe behaviour, record it, look for patterns in the observed behaviour and then make sense of it. In most cases, observations are conducted in a natural, real-world environment, where the people being monitored are unaware of the fact that their behaviour is being recorded. This is called naturalist observation.

Participant observation involves the researcher becoming part of the group whose behaviour is being observed and monitored. This may be done either with or without the participants' knowledge.

Structured (systematic) observation involves the use of an explicitly designed coding framework/chart for recording behaviour.

Controlled observation involves the recording of spontaneously occurring behaviour under conditions contrived by the researcher. Such observations usually take place in a laboratory.

Observers use systematic methods such as *event sampling* (which involves observing and recording a specific event every time it occurs) or *time sampling* (which involves observing behaviour for/at certain periods).

Strengths of observations

✔ What people say they do is often different to what they actually do, so observations give a different take on behaviour.
✔ A means of conducting preliminary investigations in a new area of research, to produce hypotheses for future investigations.
✔ Able to capture spontaneous and unexpected behaviour.
✔ Frequently high in ecological validity.
✔ Pre-prepared coding systems make the recording of behaviour easier.

Weaknesses of observations

✘ Observers may 'see' what they expect to see (observer bias).
✘ Poorly designed behaviour checklists reduce reliability (low inter-rater reliability).
✘ If participants do not know they are being observed, there are ethical problems, such as deception and invasion of privacy. If participants do know they are being observed, they may alter their behaviour (demand characteristics/ social desirability response).
✘ Observations cannot provide information about what people think or feel.

Strengths of correlations

✔ Uses quantifiable measures of each of the two variables.
✔ Gives information about the relationship between two variables.
✔ Strong correlations (positive or negative) can form the basis for further experimental research to establish cause and effect.

Correlations

Strictly speaking, correlation is a technique for data analysis rather than a research method.

Correlation is used to establish whether there is a relationship between two variables. It involves the measurement of two variables and does not involve any manipulation. It is therefore a very useful technique when variables cannot be manipulated for either practical or ethical reasons.

As individuals get older (some people like to think!), they become more beautiful. This is known as a positive correlation because the two variables increase together. On the other hand, you may disagree and think that as people get older they become less attractive. You think age and beauty are correlated (there is a relationship between the two), but it is a negative correlation: as one variable increases, the other decreases. Or you may simply feel that there is no relationship between age and beauty, in which case you would predict a zero correlation.

Weaknesses of correlations

✘ Cause and effect cannot be established.
✘ Findings can be misleading, as they can imply cause-and-effect relationships that do not actually exist.

WHAT YOU SHOULD BE ABLE TO DO IN RELATION TO THE FOUR TECHNIQUES

What you should know in relation to self-reports

- Be able to describe the terms: self-report, interview, questionnaire, survey.
- Know strengths and weakness of: self-reports in general, and interviews, questionnaires and surveys specifically.
- Be able to describe the terms: open/open-ended questions, closed/closed-ended questions.
- Know strengths and weaknesses of both open and closed questions.
- Be able to describe the term rating scale. Useful also to be able to describe: Likert scale, visual analogue scale, box scale, verbal rating scale.
- Know strengths and weaknesses of rating scales in general.

What you should be able to do in relation to the four techniques

- Identify strengths and weaknesses of the four techniques, both in general and in relation to specific source material.
- Frame hypotheses (null, alternate, one-tailed, two-tailed).
- Identify variables:
  - For experiments, identify and explain the difference between independent and dependent variables.
- Suggest how variables might be operationalised/measured.
- Suggest (in relation to source material) strengths and weakness of measurement and alternative forms of measurement.
- Comment on the reliability and validity of measurement.
- Describe opportunity sampling, random sampling and self-selected (volunteer) sampling techniques.

Experiments

- Be able to describe the terms: laboratory experiment, field experiment.
- Know strengths and weaknesses of laboratory and field experiments.
- Be able to describe the terms: dependent variable (DV), independent variable (IV).
- Be able to operationalise dependent and independent variables.
- Be able to describe the terms: extraneous variable(s), confounding variable(s).
- Be able to suggest extraneous variables and consider how they might be controlled.
- Be able to describe the terms: independent measures design (IMD), repeated measures design (RMD), matched subjects/pairs design (MSD).
- Know strengths and weaknesses of independent measures, repeated measures and matched subjects/pairs designs.

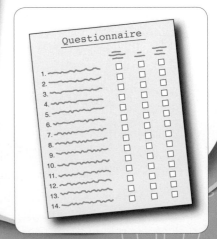

▲ **Figure 2.1** Questionnaires are a self-report technique

Observations

- Be able to describe the terms: participant observation, structured observation. Useful also to be able to describe: naturalistic observation, controlled observation.
- Know strengths and weaknesses of observations in general, and participant and structured observation specifically.
- Be able to describe the terms: time sampling, event sampling.
- Know strengths and weaknesses of time and event behaviour sampling techniques.

▲ **Figure 2.2**

- Identify strengths and weaknesses of opportunity, random and self-selecting (volunteer) sampling techniques.
- Identify strengths and weaknesses of sampling techniques described in source material.
- Suggest appropriate samples/sampling techniques in relation to source material.
- Suggest appropriate procedures in relation to source material.
- Identify and describe the differences between qualitative and quantitative data.
- Identify strengths and weaknesses of qualitative and quantitative data.
- Suggest appropriate descriptive statistics for data in source material (mean, median, mode).
- Sketch appropriate summary tables/graphs from data in source material (bar charts, scattergraphs).
- Draw conclusions from data/graphs.
- Describe ethical issues relating to psychological research with human participants.
- Identify ethical issues in source material and suggest ways of dealing with ethical issues.

Correlations

- Know and understand what a positive, negative and zero correlation is.
- Be able to describe a positive, negative and zero correlation.
- Be able to draw and label a scattergraph, showing the relationship between two variables.
- Be able to interpret information shown in scattergraphs.
- Know strengths and weaknesses of correlations.
- Identify the variables either as represented on a scattergraph or by drawing and labelling a scattergraph.
- The reliability and validity of scattergraphs.
- Draw conclusions from scattergraphs.

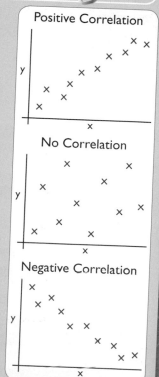

▲ **Figure 2.3**

SCENARIOS FOR THE SELF-REPORT TECHNIQUE

Scenario 1

A school librarian asked pupils to complete a questionnaire about the types of books they would like to see in the school's fiction library. Pupils were asked to select three fictional categories. The school had a population of 500 pupils, 40 of whom returned a completed questionnaire to the librarian. The findings are shown below.

▼ Table 2.1

Fictional category	Number of pupils
Science fiction	20
Fantasy	20
Crime	15
Thrillers	12
War	10
Romance	15
Historical	10
Humour	18

▼ Figure 2.4

Scenario 2

A large supermarket has decided to modernise its premises. The manager proposes to conduct a survey, asking customers what sort of refreshment/eating and drinking facilities they would like in the updated store. The survey will gather quantitative data.

Scenario 3

A researcher used a structured interview to investigate people's holiday preferences. He used open and closed questions to gather both quantitative and qualitative data about where people preferred to go on holiday, what type of holiday they enjoyed the most, and what type of accommodation suited them best.

Scenario 4

An office manager wanted to compare people's happiness levels on Monday mornings with their happiness levels on Friday mornings, to see if the thought of coming to work for the next five days influenced their mood more than the thought of the forthcoming weekend break. She decided to do this using a questionnaire in which participants had to apply a rating scale to reflect their levels of happiness.

EXAM-STYLE QUESTIONS LINKED TO THE SELF-REPORT SCENARIOS

Scenario 1

1 (a) Sketch an appropriate graph to represent the findings of this study. **[3]**

1 (b) Draw **one** conclusion from the findings of this study. **[2]**

2 Suggest why the findings of this study may not be valid. **[3]**

3 (a) Suggest how the librarian could have obtained a random sample for this study. **[3]**

(b) Describe **one** strength of using random sampling in this study. **[3]**

4 Outline an alternative way the librarian could have measured the pupils' fictional book preferences. **[6]**

Scenario 2

1 (a) Sketch an appropriate chart for recording the findings of this study. **[4]**

1 (b) Describe **one** limitation of the quantitative data that will be recorded on this chart. **[2]**

2 Identify **two** ethical issues the manager needs to consider when conducting this survey, and suggest how they could be managed. **[6]**

3 Outline an appropriate procedure the manager could follow for this study. **[8]**

Scenario 3

1 (a) Describe the terms 'open question' and 'closed question'. **[4]**

(b) Give an appropriate 'open question' that could have been used in this study. **[2]**

2 (a) Describe a sampling technique the researcher could have used to obtain a suitable sample in this study. **[2]**

(b) Describe **one** strength of using this sampling technique for this study. **[2]**

3 Discuss the issues of reliability **and** validity in relation to this study. **[10]**

Scenario 4

1 (a) Describe an appropriate rating scale for this study. **[3]**

(b) Outline **one** weakness of using a rating scale in this study. **[2]**

2 (a) Describe the type of data gathered in this study. **[2]**

(b) Outline **one** strength of this type of data in relation to this study. **[2]**

3 (a) Suggest an appropriate alternate one-tailed hypothesis for this study. **[3]**

(b) Explain what makes your hypothesis one-tailed. **[2]**

4 Briefly discuss the issue of reliability in relation to this study. **[6]**

SCENARIOS FOR THE EXPERIMENTAL TECHNIQUE

Scenario 1

A researcher decided to investigate who could type text messages on mobile phones faster – boys or girls. She decided to do this using a laboratory experiment.

▼ **Figure 2.5**

Scenario 2

A physical education teacher used a field experiment with a repeated measures design to measure the effect of wearing a swimming cap on the performance of the boys in his school swimming team. All the boys improved their performance over 50 metres when swimming front crawl. Results are shown below.

▼ Table 2.2

Participant	Improvement in seconds
LB	5
GT	3
SD	3
JK	I
VH	2
JA	4
WS	3

Scenario 3

A primary schoolteacher wanted to find out whether pupils in his Year 6 class learn spellings better in the morning or the afternoon. Therefore he decided to do an experiment using an independent measures design, in which half the class were tested at 10.00am and the other half at 3.00pm. Each participant was given 5 minutes to learn the same 12 unassociated words before being tested to see how many they could spell correctly.

Scenario 4

Several university students complained to their lecturer that the white background of the interactive whiteboard was giving them headaches, which made it difficult for them to copy information quickly. The lecturer therefore suggested that he conduct an experiment to see which background colour – yellow, green, blue, purple or pink – resulted in the students copying down writing from the board the quickest.

EXAM-STYLE QUESTIONS LINKED TO THE EXPERIMENTAL SCENARIOS

Scenario 1

1 (a) Suggest a null hypothesis for this investigation. **[2]**

   (b) Identify the independent variable (IV) **and** dependent variable (DV) in this study. **[2]**

2 (a) Describe the term 'laboratory experiment'. **[2]**

   (b) Outline **one** strength of using a laboratory experiment for this study. **[2]**

   (c) Outline **one** weakness of using a laboratory experiment for this study. **[2]**

3 Describe an appropriate procedure for this experiment. **[10]**

Scenario 2

1 (a) Suggest an appropriate two-tailed experimental hypothesis for this study. **[2]**

   (b) Explain what makes your hypothesis two-tailed. **[2]**

2 (a) Calculate the mean **and** modal times for the participants in this study. **[4]**

   (b) Describe **one** advantage of knowing the modal time of the participants in this study. **[2]**

3 (a) Describe the term 'repeated measures design'. **[2]**

   (b) Outline **one** disadvantage of using a repeated measures design in this study. **[2]**

4 Describe **two** extraneous variables that could have influenced the findings of this study. **[4]**

Scenario 3

1 (a) Describe the term 'independent measures design'. **[2]**

   (b) Outline **one** strength of using an independent measures design in this study. **[2]**

2 (a) Describe **two** controls the teacher could have included in his experiment. **[6]**

   (b) Explain the value of having controls in psychological investigations. **[2]**

3 (a) Consider the extent to which this study has ecological validity. **[4]**

   (b) Describe **two** ways in which the ecological validity of this study could have been increased. **[4]**

Scenario 4

1 (a) Formulate an appropriate experimental hypothesis for this study. **[2]**

   (b) Identify the independent variable (IV) **and** the dependent variable (DV) in this study. **[2]**

2 Identify **two** ethical issues the lecturer should consider before conducting this experiment, and suggest how he could manage them. **[4]**

3 Outline **one** extraneous variable that could influence the findings of this study. **[2]**

4 Describe an appropriate procedure for this experiment. **[10]**

SCENARIOS FOR THE OBSERVATIONAL TECHNIQUE

Scenario 1

Many disabled people complained to the manager of a 24-hour shopping complex that every time they visited the centre their designated parking spaces were occupied by cars not displaying an appropriate disabled certificate. The manager therefore decided to conduct an observation to find out if there were specific times of the day when this issue was particularly problematic. He might then be able to put measures in place to alleviate the situation.

Scenario 3

A practice manager was looking for ways to cut expenditure. Therefore she decided to find out which magazines/journals patients preferred to read while waiting for a consultation with their doctor. The findings would mean she could save the practice money by only purchasing the most popular publications. She bought several copies of 12 different magazines and placed them on tables around the practice consulting room. She gathered her data using participant observation.

Scenario 2

The owner of a several pubs read in a newspaper that men are more likely than women to gamble on fruit machines in entertainment arcades. He was curious to find out if a similar trend existed in his pubs. Therefore he decided to conduct an observation, using the event sampling technique, to find out whether more men or more women used the fruit machines in his pubs.

▼ **Figure 2.6**

Scenario 4

The head teacher of a small sixth-form college wanted to find out what his students did when allowed to spend time in the common room. He therefore designed a coding chart and asked two of his senior students to conduct a covert observation, at convenient times throughout the week prior to half-term. Their findings are shown below.

▼ Table 2.3

Behavioural categories	Number of students
Studying	8
Using mobile phone/iPod, etc.	50
Self-grooming (doing hair/make-up, etc.)	20
Sleeping	6
Eating/preparing food or drink	40
Watching TV	60
Playing games on a computer	50
Playing cards/board games	10

EXAM-STYLE QUESTIONS LINKED TO THE OBSERVATIONAL SCENARIOS

Scenario 1

1 (a) Suggest how the shopping complex's manager could have gathered appropriate data using the time sampling technique. **[4]**

(b) Describe **one** weakness of the time sampling technique for gathering data in this study. **[2]**

2 (a) Describe the type of data gathered in this study. **[2]**

(b) Outline **one** weakness of this type of data in relation to this study. **[2]**

3 Outline an appropriate procedure for this study. **[10]**

Scenario 2

1 (a) Describe the term 'event sampling'. **[2]**

(b) Outline how the owner of the pubs could have gathered appropriate data in this study using the event sampling technique. **[4]**

2 (a) Formulate an appropriate one-tailed hypothesis for this study. **[2]**

(b) Explain what makes your hypothesis one-tailed. **[2]**

3 Discuss the issues of reliability and validity in relation to this study. **[10]**

Scenario 3

1 (a) Describe the term 'participant observation' in relation to this study. **[4]**

(b) Describe **one** strength of using participant observation in this study. **[2]**

(c) Describe **one** weakness of using participant observation in this study. **[2]**

2 (a) Sketch a possible coding/observation chart for this study. **[4]**

(b) Describe **two** ways in which the findings from this observation could be displayed. **[4]**

3 (a) Describe the opportunity sampling technique in relation to this study. **[2]**

(b) Describe **one** weakness of the opportunity sampling technique in relation to this study. **[2]**

Scenario 4

1 (a) Sketch an appropriate graph to represent the findings of this study. **[3]**

(b) Draw **one** conclusion from the findings of this observation. **[2]**

2 (a) Describe **one** strength of using the observational technique to gather data in this study. **[2]**

(b) Describe **one** weakness of using the observational technique to gather data in this study. **[2]**

(c) Outline an alternative way data could have been gathered for this study. **[2]**

3 Describe **two** ethical issues the head teacher had to consider when conducting this investigation. **[4]**

4 Briefly discuss the issue of reliability in relation to this study. **[5]**

SCENARIOS FOR THE CORRELATIONAL TECHNIQUE

Scenario 1

A researcher decided to investigate whether there is a relationship between how much coffee people drink at breakfast and their reaction time. He anticipated that the findings would show a negative correlation.

Scenario 3

A psychologist wants to investigate whether there is a correlation between an individual's monthly earnings/income and the amount of money they spend each month on mobile phone usage.

Scenario 2

An occupational therapist wanted to investigate whether there is a relationship between age and physical recreation. She therefore advertised in a local newspaper for participants between the ages of 18 and 80 years to contact her, so she could send them a lifestyle questionnaire to complete. A critical question in the questionnaire measured the average time spent each week by the participant doing some form of physical activity, and there was a box at the top of the questionnaire in which the participant was asked to state their age. The findings are shown below.

▼ Table 2.4

Age range of participants (years)	Mean time spent by each participant per week doing a physical activity (minutes)
18–25	120
26–35	100
36–45	30
46–55	90
56–65	75
66–75	60
76–80	40

Scenario 4

A researcher decided to investigate the relationship between perceived stress levels and the amount of time spent watching television. He first asked participants to complete a questionnaire to assess stress levels and then to estimate how many hours of television they watched each day. The findings are shown in the scattergraph below.

▼ **Figure 2.7** Participants' stress scores

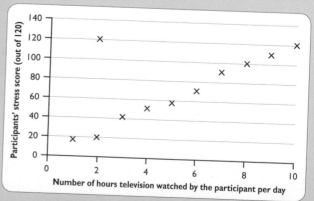

EXAM-STYLE QUESTIONS LINKED TO THE CORRELATIONAL SCENARIOS

Scenario 1

1 (a) Describe the term 'negative correlation' in relation to this study. **[2]**

1 (b) Formulate an appropriate alternative hypothesis for this investigation. **[2]**

2 (a) Identify **two** extraneous variables that could influence the findings of this study. **[2]**

   (b) Outline how **one** extraneous variable could be controlled in this investigation. **[2]**

3 (a) Describe an appropriate sampling technique that could be used to gather participants for this study. **[2]**

   (b) Outline **one** weakness of your proposed sampling technique. **[2]**

4 Outline how the researcher could have conducted this study. **[8]**

Scenario 2

1 (a) Sketch a scattergraph to show the findings of this study. **[3]**

   (b) Draw **two** conclusions from this scattergraph. **[4]**

2 (a) Describe the sampling technique used in this study. **[2]**

   (b) Suggest **one** strength of using this sampling technique in this study. **[2]**

3 (a) Describe **one** way in which time spent doing physical activity per week could have been measured in this study. **[3]**

   (b) Outline **one** weakness of your suggested way of measuring participation in physical activity. **[2]**

4 Describe **one** practical problem the occupational therapist may have encountered with this study. **[4]**

Scenario 3

1 (a) Describe the term 'correlation' in relation to this study. **[2]**

   (b) Formulate an appropriate hypothesis for this study. **[2]**

   (c) Identify the **two** variables being measured in this study. **[2]**

2 Describe **one** ethical issue the psychologist needs to consider in relation to this study, and suggest how it might be managed. **[4]**

3 Describe an appropriate procedure for this study. **[10]**

Scenario 4

1 (a) Describe **one** strength of correlations. **[2]**

   (b) Describe **one** weakness of correlations. **[2]**

2 (a) Describe the correlation shown in the scattergraph. **[2]**

   (b) Suggest **one** conclusion that could be drawn from this scattergraph. **[2]**

   (c) Sketch an appropriate table, showing the findings of this investigation. **[4]**

3 (a) Describe **one** disadvantage of using a questionnaire to measure stress levels. **[2]**

   (b) Suggest an alternative way stress levels could have been measured in this study. **[2]**

4 Briefly discuss the issue of validity in relation to this investigation. **[4]**

LOFTUS AND PALMER (1974): EYEWITNESS TESTIMONY

Reconstruction of automobile destruction

Theory/ies on which the study is based

- Schema theory proposes that memory is influenced by what an individual already knows, and that their use of past experience to deal with a new experience is a fundamental feature of the way the human mind works.

- Knowledge is stored in memory as a set of schemas – simplified, generalised mental representations of everything an individual understands by a given type of object or event, based on their past experiences.

- The schema forms part of Bartlett's theory of reconstructive memory, which forms the basis for Loftus and Palmer's study into EWT.

Background to the study

- Memory involves interpreting what is seen or heard, recording bits of it, and then reconstructing these bits into memories when required.

- This implies that recall can be distorted or biased by certain features of the situation.

- Loftus and Palmer conducted many studies investigating ways in which memory can be distorted, many of which show that EWT is highly unreliable because it can be influenced by such things as subtle differences in the wording of questions.

- This study focuses on the effects of 'leading questions' on an individual's ability to remember events accurately.

- The expectation was that any information subtly introduced after the event through leading questions (questions phrased in a way that suggests the expected answer) would distort the original memory.

Relation to the cognitive approach

- Cognitive processes include how we attain, retain and regain information, through the processes of perception, attention, memory, problem-solving, decision-making, language and thought.

- This study is concerned with eyewitness testimony (EWT) and shows that memory is reconstructive.

- Bartlett's (1932) theory of reconstructive memory proposes that individuals reconstruct the past by fitting new information into their existing understanding of the world – a schema.

- Loftus and Palmer showed that EWT is influenced by people's tendency to reconstruct their memories of events to fit their schemas.

▲ Figure 3.1

Research method

Experiment 1

- This was a laboratory experiment using an independent measures design.
- The independent variable (IV) was the wording of a critical question hidden in a questionnaire. This question asked: 'About how fast were the cars going when they hit/smashed/collided/contacted/bumped each other?'
- The dependent variable (DV) was the estimated speed given by the participant.

Experiment 2

- This was also a laboratory experiment using an independent measures design.
- The independent variable (IV) was the wording of a question in a questionnaire:
  - One group was asked: 'About how fast were the cars going when they smashed into each other?'
  - A second group was asked: 'About how fast were the cars going when they hit each other?'
  - A third group was not asked about speed.
- One week later, all participants were asked to complete another questionnaire, which contained the critical question, 'Did you see any broken glass?'
- The dependent variable (DV) was whether the answer to this question was, 'Yes/No'.

Outline of the procedure/study

Experiment 1

- Forty-five students were divided into five groups, with nine participants in each group.
- All participants were shown the same seven film clips of different traffic accidents, which were originally made as part of a driver safety film.
- After each clip, participants were given a questionnaire, which asked them first to describe the accident and then to answer a series of questions about the accident.
- There was one critical question in the questionnaire: 'About how fast were the cars going when they hit each other?'
- One group was given this question, while the other four were given the verbs 'smashed', 'collided', 'contacted' or 'bumped', instead of 'hit'.

Experiment 2

- One hundred and fifty students were divided into three groups.
- All participants were shown a 1-minute film, which contained a 4-second multiple car crash.
- They were then given a questionnaire, which asked them to describe the accident and answer a set of questions about the incident.
- There was a critical question about speed:
  - One group was asked: 'About how fast were the cars going when they smashed into each other?'
  - Another group was asked: 'About how fast were the cars going when they hit each other?'
  - The third group did not have a question about vehicular speed.
- One week later, all participants, without seeing the film again, completed another questionnaire about the accident, which contained the further critical question: 'Did you see any broken glass – Yes/No?' There had been no broken glass in the original film.

Key findings

Experiment 1

Speed estimates for the verbs used in the critical question are shown in Table 3.1.

▼ Table 3.1

Verb	Mean speed estimate (mph)
Smashed	40.8
Collided	39.3
Bumped	38.1
Hit	34.0
Contacted	31.8

'Smashed' produced the fastest speed estimates and 'contacted' the slowest.

For the four staged films where speeds were accurately measured:

- The film of a crash at 20 mph was estimated to be 37.7 mph.
- The film of a crash at 30 mph was estimated to be 36.2 mph.
- The films of crashes at 40 mph were estimated to be 39.7 mph and 36.1 mph.

Experiment 2

Speed estimates for the verbs used in the question about speed are shown in Table 3.2.

▼ Table 3.2

Verb	Mean speed estimate (mph)
Smashed	10.46
Hit	8.00

'Smashed' produced the highest speed estimates.

Responses to the question, 'Did you see any broken glass?' are shown in Table 3.3.

▼ Table 3.3

Response	Smashed	Hit	Control
Yes	16	7	6
No	34	43	44

More participants in the 'smashed' condition than either the 'hit' or control groups reported seeing broken glass. The majority of participants in each group correctly recalled that they had not seen any broken glass.

Conclusions

- The verb used in a question influences a participant's response – that is, the way a question is phrased influences the answer given.
- People are not very good at judging vehicular speed.

Usefulness

- Based on findings such as these, the Devlin report (1976) recommended that trial judges be required to instruct the jury that it is not safe to convict on a single eyewitness testimony, except in exceptional circumstances or when there is substantial corroborative evidence.
- The recommendation was rejected by the judiciary and the Home Office, but juries are now warned of the dangers of honest mistakes by eyewitnesses.

▲ Figure 3.2

Issues to be considered

- Strengths/weaknesses of the research method.
- Strengths/weaknesses of an independent measures design.
- Strengths/weaknesses of snapshot studies.
- Strengths/weaknesses of the sample.
- Strengths/weaknesses of quantitative data.
- Reliability.
- Validity and ecological validity.
- Ethics.

Exam tips for this study

- Know there are two separate experiments and the procedure followed for each one.
- Know the key findings for each experiment.
- Be able to draw conclusions from the findings.
- Be able to suggest at least one way in which the study could be improved, and possible implications of the suggestion(s) for methodology, ethics, reliability, validity, usefulness, practicality, and so on.

Exam-style questions linked to this study

Section A

1 Describe the sample used in the study. **[2]**
2 **(a)** Identify the independent variable (IV) in Experiment 1. **[2]**
   (b) Outline how the independent variable (IV) was manipulated in Experiment 1. **[2]**
3 Outline **two** ways in which the procedure was standardised. **[4]**
4 Outline **two** ways in which this study lacked ecological validity. **[4]**
5 **(a)** Give **one** finding from Experiment 2. **[2]**
   (b) Outline **one** conclusion that can be drawn from the findings of Experiment 2. **[2]**
6 Describe how **two** ethical concerns were managed in these experiments. **[4]**

Section B

(a) Briefly outline the research method used in this study. **[2]**
(b) Explain why this study can be considered a snapshot study. **[4]**
(c) With reference to this study, describe **one** strength and **one** weakness of snapshot studies. **[6]**
(d) Describe the procedure used in this study. **[8]**
(e) Describe how this study could be improved. **[8]**
(f) Outline the implications of the procedural changes you have suggested. **[8]**

Section C

(a) Outline **one** assumption of the cognitive approach. **[2]**
(b) With reference to this study, describe how the cognitive approach might explain the inaccuracy of eyewitness testimony. **[4]**
(c) Describe **one** similarity and **one** difference between this and one other core study that takes the cognitive approach. **[6]**
(d) Discuss strengths **and** weaknesses of the cognitive approach, using examples from this and any other core studies that take the cognitive approach. **[12]**

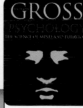

GROSS
PSYCHOLOGY
THE SCIENCE OF MIND AND BEHAVIOUR

pp. 3, 319–22

BARON-COHEN *ET AL.* (1997): ADULTS WITH AUTISM AND THEORY OF MIND

Another advanced test of theory of mind: Evidence from very high functioning adults with autism or Asperger syndrome

Background to the study

- Some evidence suggests that a theory of mind (ToM) deficit is not a core cognitive deficit in autism.

- But no conclusive evidence has yet shown that individuals such as adults with high-functioning autism or Asperger's syndrome have an intact ToM. This is because usual tests to assess ToM have a ceiling in developmental terms, corresponding to a mental age of about 6 years. Therefore, although existing ToM tests are challenging for 6-year-olds, they are far too easy for adults, who all pass, even though they may not have a fully functioning ToM.

- Happé (1994) tested adults with autism or Asperger's syndrome on an 'advanced' ToM task, and found that her participants had more difficulty with her mental state stories (Happé's Strange Stories) than matched controls.

- Baron-Cohen *et al.* built on Happé's research by using an adult test to assess theory-of-mind competence in high-functioning adults with autism or AS.

Relation to the cognitive approach

- Autism is a cognitive disorder that develops throughout childhood, but is very difficult to diagnose before the age of 3 years.

- The cognitive approach could therefore explain the difficulties experienced by individuals with autism, because they seem to have a core cognitive deficit – an impaired theory of mind – which leaves them with social, communicative and imaginative abnormalities.

- For example, in this study by Baron-Cohen *et al.*, adults with autism/Asperger's syndrome (AS) were significantly less able to cope with the Eyes Task (an advanced test for theory of mind) than either 'normal' adults or adults with Tourette's syndrome. Not being able to read emotions from eyes may explain why those with autism have difficulty inferring mental states in other people.

Theory/ies on which the study is based

- The most influential theory of autism in recent years maintains that what all autistic people have in common (the core deficit) is *mind-blindness* (Baron Cohen, 1990), a severe impairment in their understanding of mental states and in their appreciation of how mental states govern behaviour. They lack a theory of mind (ToM).

- Because autistic individuals fail to develop the ability to attribute mental states to other people, fundamental implications arise for communication, where making sense of others' intentions enables the listener to understand what is being said (inferred/intended) (Baron-Cohen, 1995a).

- Individuals diagnosed with autism show a tremendous variation in the degree to which they are affected. To address this issue, a 'spectrum of autism' was devised. Difficulties experienced by children, judged in relation to set criteria, allow them to be placed within the spectrum e.g.

Classic autism	*Asperger's syndrome*	*Normality*

▲ **Figure 3.3**

(Those with Asperger's syndrome show the same characteristics as autism, but are of average or above-average intelligence and appear to have good communication skills, though this may not actually be the case.)

Research method

- This was a quasi/natural experiment, because the independent variable (the type of person likely to have ToM deficits – adults with high-functioning autism/AS, normal adults and adults with Tourette's syndrome (TS)) was naturally occurring, so could not be manipulated or controlled by the researchers. The dependent variable was the performance (score out of 25) on the Eyes Task, measured by showing each participant 25 black and white, standardised photographs of the eye region of faces (male and female), and asking them to make a forced choice between two mental-state words (target and foil) to best describe what the person in the photograph was feeling or thinking.

- The study used a matched participants design because the group of normal adults and the group with TS were age-matched with the group of adults with autism/AS.

Outline of the procedure/study

- Three groups of participants were tested:
  - Group 1: 16 individuals with high-functioning autism or Asperger's syndrome (high-functioning autism = 4, AS = 12). The sex ratio was 13:3 (m:f). All were of normal intelligence and were recruited through an advert in the magazine of the National Autistic Society and a variety of clinical sources.
  - Group 2: 50 normal age-matched adults, drawn from the general population of Cambridge. The sex ratio was 25:25 (m:f).
  - Group 3: 10 adults with Tourette's syndrome, also age-matched with groups 1 and 2. The sex ratio was 8:2 (m:f). All were of normal intelligence and were recruited from a tertiary referral centre in London.

- The Eyes Task, the Strange Stories Task and the two control tasks (Gender Recognition of Eyes Task, Basic Emotion Recognition Task) were presented in random order to all participants.

- The Gender Recognition of Eyes Task involved identifying the gender of the eyes used in the Eyes Task. The task controlled for face perception, perceptual discrimination and social perception. The Basic Emotion Recognition Task involved judging photographs of whole faces displaying basic emotions identified by Ekman (1992). The task was done to check whether difficulties on the Eyes Task were due to difficulties with basic emotional recognition. The Strange Stories Task was used to validate the results from the Eyes Task.

- Participants were tested individually in a quiet room, either in their own home, in the researchers' clinic or in the researchers' laboratory at Cambridge University.

Conclusions

● Contrary to previous research with adults, these results seem to provide evidence that adults with autism/AS do possess an impaired theory of mind.

● As some of the autism/AS group hold university degrees, it is reasonable to suggest that ToM deficits are independent of general intelligence.

Key findings

▼ **Table 3.4** Results of the Eyes Task (out of 25)

	Mean score	Range
Autistic/AS	16.3	13–23
Normal	20.3	16–25
TS	20.4	16–25

● The mean score for adults with TS (20.4) was not significantly different from normal adults (20.3), but both were significantly higher than the autism/AS mean score (16.3).

● Normal females performed significantly better than normal males on the Eyes Task (mean 21.8 versus 18.8), but the normal males were significantly better than the autism/AS group (mean 18.8 versus 16.3).

● The autism/AS group made significantly more errors on the Strange Stories Task than either of the other groups.

● On the gender and emotion control tasks, there were no differences between the groups.

● Within the autism/AS group there was no significant correlation between IQ and performance on the Eyes Task.

▲ **Figure 3.4** Some of the expressions participants were asked about in the experiment

Usefulness

● The study allows further understanding of the extent of the problem of theory of mind across the autistic spectrum, and shows that the problem extends beyond childhood into adulthood. Such knowledge allows us to be more empathetic towards not only autistic children, but also adults placed on the autistic spectrum.

● The study shows that lacking a ToM seems unrelated to general levels of intelligence, and is significantly more prevalent in individuals with autism than individuals with other forms of impaired cognitive development (i.e. those with Tourette's syndrome). This knowledge allows appropriate techniques to be developed to encourage both ToM skills and interaction with autistic people.

● Many techniques to assist people on the autistic spectrum to develop effective social skills have already been developed – for example, Temple Grandin developed strategies to understand and predict the thoughts and behaviours of others. Such work is ongoing, and any research, such as this study, that can shed additional light on the difficulties experienced by autistic people will enhance the development of appropriate remedial and therapeutic techniques.

Issues to be considered

- Strengths/weaknesses of laboratory experiments.
- Strengths/weaknesses of snapshot studies.
- Strengths/weaknesses of quantitative data.
- Strengths/weaknesses of the sample.
- Reliability.
- Validity and ecological validity.
- Ethics.

Exam tips for this study

- Know the features of all three groups of participants and how each group was gathered.
- Know the research method.
- Be able to describe the Eyes Task and the two control tasks.
- Know why the Strange Stories Task and the control tasks were used.
- Be able to outline the procedure.
- Know the key findings.
- Be able to draw conclusions from the findings.
- Be able to suggest at least one way in which the study could be improved, and possible implications of the suggestion(s) for methodology, ethics, reliability, validity, usefulness, practicality, and so on.

Exam-style questions linked to this study

Section A

1 With reference to this study, describe the term Theory of Mind. **[4]**

2 (a) Identify the **two** control groups in this study. **[2]**

  (b) Outline why **one** of the control groups was used in this study. **[2]**

3 (a) Identify the **two** control tasks used in this study. **[2]**

  (b) Describe how **one** of the control tasks was conducted in this study. **[2]**

4 Describe the Eyes Task as used in this study. **[4]**

5 Describe what is meant by a target word and a foil word in relation to this study. **[4]**

6 Using the chart below, outline **two** findings from this study. **[4]**

▼ **Table 3.5** Results of the Eyes Task (out of 25)

	Mean score	**Range**
Autistic/AS	16.3	13–23
Normal	20.3	16–25
TS	20.4	16–25

Section B

(a) Outline why this study was conducted. **[2]**

(b) Describe why this study can be considered a laboratory experiment. **[4]**

(c) With reference to this study, suggest **one** strength and **one** weakness of laboratory experiments. **[6]**

(d) Describe the findings of this study. **[8]**

(e) Suggest ways in which this study could be improved. **[8]**

(f) Consider the implications of the improvements you have suggested. **[8]**

Section C

(a) Outline **one** implication of the cognitive approach. **[2]**

(b) With reference to this study, describe how the cognitive approach could explain autism.

(c) Describe **one** similarity and **one** difference between any of the core studies that take the cognitive approach. **[6]**

(d) Discuss strengths **and** weaknesses of the cognitive approach, using examples from any of the core studies that take this approach. **[12]**

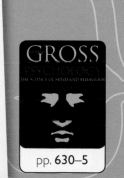

GROSS
PSYCHOLOGY
THE SCIENCE OF MIND AND BEHAVIOUR

pp. 630–5

SAVAGE-RUMBAUGH *ET AL.* (1986): APE LANGUAGE

Spontaneous symbol acquisition and communication in pygmy chimpanzees (pan paniscus)

▲ **Figure 3.5** Kanzi

Background to the study

- The ability of apes to acquire language has been the focus of a number of research projects – for example, Vicky (Hayes and Hayes, 1952); Gua (Kellogg and Kellogg, 1933); Washoe (Gardner and Gardner, 1969); Sarah (Premack and Premack, 1983).

- Although the various projects utilised different communicative systems (e.g. American Sign Language, geometric symbols, plastic tokens), in general, all have found that apes can learn to produce symbols in order to gain desired consequences.

- Research has also shown that when a chimpanzee is systematically taught the skills of requesting, labelling and comprehending, s/he will use symbols without further training to make request-oriented utterances and statements about behaviour s/he intends to engage in, and to orient people's attention to aspects of the environment other than the mere fulfilment of immediate needs (Savage-Rumbaugh, 1984b, 1986; Savage-Rumbaugh *et al.* 1983).

Relation to the cognitive approach

- As cognitive psychology involves the study of all mental processes, this approach considers methods of communication and language acquisition. Communication can be between humans, between animals, or between humans and animals.

- Savage-Rumbaugh et al. studied four chimpanzees – Kanzi and Mulika (pygmy chimpanzees) and Austin and Sherman (common chimpanzees) – and found that they spontaneously acquired symbol use through observation, and were able to communicate with humans using language in the form of lexigrams.

- She found the pygmy chimpanzees to have a greater propensity for the acquisition of symbols than common chimpanzees; and, although their ability to acquire language seems more limited than that of humans, they are able to learn enough aspects to communicate with humans at a basic level.

Theory/ies on which the study is based

- Chomsky (1957) and Lenneberg (1967) believe language is a species-specific behaviour that is common, but unique, to all humans.

- Lock (1980) identified two stages in language learning: associative symbol learning and representational (referential) symbol learning.

- It is generally agreed that language development in humans follows a universal timetable – that is, all children pass through the same sequence of stages at approximately the same ages –though developmental rate may vary. There are three main stages: prelinguistic stage, one-word stage, two-word sentence stage.

- There is a difference between the ability to produce language and the ability to comprehend language. Savage-Rumbaugh *et al.* focused on the ability to comprehend language.

Research method

- Savage-Rumbaugh states: 'What follows is not an experiment but rather a description of events'. This study is therefore generally described as a longitudinal case study. The in-depth, very detailed data gathered in relation to the symbol acquisition and communicative use by Kanzi, in particular, and, to a lesser extent, Mulika, Austin and Sherman, mean the research can be considered a case study.

- As the report describes the development of these phenomena over a period of 17 months, the study can be considered longitudinal.

- The participants were:
  - Kanzi – a pygmy chimpanzee born in captivity to Matata;
  - Mulika – Kanzi's younger sister;
  - Austin and Sherman – two common chimpanzees, given formal language training on the same system from ages 1.5 and 2.5 years respectively.

- Savage-Rumbaugh *et al.* set out to investigate language acquisition in pygmy chimpanzees, as they argued that ape research had not, thus far, objectively demonstrated:

  - spontaneous referential symbol production without intensive training;
  - spontaneous referential symbol comprehension of spoken English;
  - referential language in pygmy chimpanzees.

- Kanzi was the prime participant because he was observed to have started using symbols spontaneously.

Outline of the procedure/study

- For 17 months, from the age of 2.5 years, Kanzi's use of a lexigram board was recorded. The lexigram board consisted of geometric visual symbols, representing words that brightened when touched. These symbols were on an electronic keyboard for indoor use, or on a pointing board for outdoor use. A speech synthesiser was added later.

- Unlike Austin and Sherman, no formal language training was given to Kanzi and Mulika, who were merely exposed to people who modelled symbol usage on the keyboard and used spoken English and gestures to describe everyday objects, activities and interactions, with the apes and with each other.

- All ape symbol usage was recorded automatically via computer when the lexigram was used indoors, and by hand when the pointing board was used outdoors – these data were then entered into the computer at the end of each day.

- Tests of language:
  - Spontaneous symbol use, verified by behaviour concordance measures on 9 out of 10 occasions, was the criterion for symbol acquisition.
  - Informal structured utterance tests assessed symbol comprehension.
  - Formal laboratory matching tests:
    - i. photograph to lexigram
    - ii. spoken English to photograph
    - iii. spoken English to lexigram
    - iv. synthesised speech to lexigram

  An additional test was the blind test of Kanzi's knowledge of the foraging sites around the 55-acre forest.

Key findings

- Kanzi and Mulika naturally used more explicit gestures to communicate than Austin and Sherman.
- Kanzi started using the lexigram when he was aged 2.5 years, while Mulika began using symbols aged 12 months.
- In total, during the period covered by this study, Kanzi acquired 46 words and Mulika 37, with Mulika's initial acquisition rate being slower than Kanzi's.
- Examples of Kanzi's symbol acquisition are shown in Table 5.1.

▼ **Table 3.6**

Age (months)	30	35	41	46
Example	Peanut	Bread	M&M	Hotdog

- Kanzi's multi-symbol utterances (combinations) appeared within the first month of spontaneous keyboard usage. In total, over the 17-month period, he produced 2,540 non-imitative combinations and 265 prompted or partially imitated combinations. All but 10 of the non-imitative combinations were judged appropriate and interpretable, and 764 were produced only once.
- About 15 per cent of Kanzi and Mulika's utterances were imitative and 80 per cent spontaneous.
- Both Kanzi and Mulika did well on the formal tests, making very few errors when matching spoken English words to the lexigram, spoken English words to photographs, and photographs to the lexigram.
- Austin and Sherman were able to match photographs to the lexigram, but struggled matching spoken English words to photographs.
- In the blind test, where Kanzi had to lead a person to a preselected location, his performance was 100 per cent correct.

Conclusions

- As Kanzi (in particular) was able to demonstrate referential symbol acquisition and spoken English comprehension without specific training, this study indicates that certain non-humans (here, pygmy chimpanzees) have linguistic abilities similar to those found in homo sapiens.
- Kanzi's language acquisition – from associative usage to referential symbols – indicates that linguistic development in pygmy chimpanzees mirrors that of humans.
- One must be cautious about making any generalisations from the findings of this study, as only four chimpanzees (two pygmy, two common) were studied.
- Further research is required, notably using chimpanzees of both species that have been reared together, to investigate the ability of non-human animals to acquire and use human language.

Usefulness

- Ape studies are of great scientific value, as they add to our understanding of our closest evolutionary species and allow us to continue to learn about our own origins.
- Findings from language acquisition, production and comprehension studies using apes have helped researchers develop ways of communication for children with special needs who are unable to speak (e.g. using a lexigram).
- Because the chimps displayed many characteristics of child language learning, findings from this study can help psychologists identify and help children who display difficulties early in the language acquisition process.

▲ **Figure 3.6** A lexigram board like the one Savage-Rumbaugh used with Kanzi

Issues to be considered

- Strengths/weaknesses of case studies.
- Strengths/weaknesses of longitudinal studies.
- Strengths/weaknesses of observation as a way to gather data.
- Strengths/weaknesses of quantitative and qualitative data.
- Strengths/weaknesses of the sample.
- Reliability.
- Validity and ecological validity.
- Ethics.

Exam tips for this study

- Know the sample and the communication system used.
- Know how both quantitative and qualitative data were gathered. Be able to give examples of both types of data.
- Know how language acquisition was assessed/tested.
- Know the key findings.
- Be able to draw conclusions from the findings.
- Be able to suggest at least one way in which the study could be improved, and possible implications of the suggestion(s) for methodology, ethics, reliability, validity, usefulness, practicality, and so on.

Exam-style questions linked to this study

Section A

1 **(a)** Identify the **two** common chimpanzees used in this study. **[2]**

  (b) Outline why common chimpanzees were used in this study. **[2]**

2 Explain why this study 'is not an experiment' (Savage-Rumbaugh *et al.*, 1986), but is better described as a longitudinal case study. **[4]**

3 Describe the communication system used in this study. **[4]**

4 Describe **two** of the formal laboratory tests given to Kanzi. **[4]**

5 Outline how Kanzi's knowledge of the foraging sites was tested. **[4]**

6 **(a)** Identify **two** pieces of quantitative data gathered in this study. **[2]**

  (b) Outline **one** piece of qualitative data gathered in this study. **[2]**

Section B

  (a) Outline **one** previous study into language acquisition ability in apes. **[4]**

  (b) Describe how quantitative data was gathered in this study. **[4]**

  (c) Outline **one** strength and **one** weakness of quantitative data as used in this study. **[6]**

  (d) Outline how observation was used in this study. **[6]**

  (e) Outline how language acquisition was assessed in this study. **[6]**

  (f) Discuss the issue of ethics in relation to this study. **[10]**

Section C

  (a) Outline the cognitive approach. **[2]**

  (b) Describe how the cognitive approach could explain language acquisition by chimpanzees. **[4]**

  (c) Describe **one** similarity and **one** difference between any of the core studies that take the cognitive approach. **[6]**

  (d) Discuss strengths **and** weaknesses of the cognitive approach, using examples from any of the core studies that take this approach. **[12]**

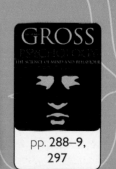

GROSS

pp. 288–9, 297

SAMUEL AND BRYANT (1984): CONSERVATION

Asking only one question in the conservation experiment

Background to the study

- Conservation experiments conducted by Piaget and Szeminska (1952) indicated that children below the age of 7 or 8 years could not conserve number.

- Donaldson (1978, 1982) suggested that conservation errors produced by many children may actually be caused by the experimenter unwittingly forcing them to produce wrong answers against their better judgement.

- Support for Donaldson's suggestion was provided by Rose and Blank (1974), who varied Piaget's traditional number conservation experiment by asking one question rather than two. This question was asked after the transformation took place in front of the child. The result was that many children who failed the traditional two-question task succeeded when asked only the post-transformation question.

Relation to the developmental approach

- Developmental psychology looks at the biological, cognitive, social and emotional changes that occur in people over time.

- As children grow up and mature mentally, their cognitive abilities develop so that they can cope with and understand increasingly complex phenomena. This was shown through this study by Samuel and Bryant, because the mean number of errors made by children in all three conditions (standard, one judgement, fixed array) decreased with age, showing that their ability to conserve became increasingly better as they got older. The study also showed that conservational abilities develop gradually as the child's cognitive abilities develop, because children were able to conserve number before they were able to conserve mass or volume.

Theory/ies on which the study is based

- Piaget proposed that cognitive development occurs through the interaction of innate capacities (nature) with environmental events (nurture), and progresses through a series of hierarchical, qualitatively different stages.

- All children pass through the stages in the same sequence, without skipping any or (except in the case of brain damage) regressing to earlier ones.

- Piaget's four stages of cognitive development are: sensorimotor (0–2 years), pre-operational (2–7 years), concrete operational (7–11 years), formal operational (11 years onwards).

- Piaget believed that pre-operational children cannot conserve and that this ability develops in the concrete operational stage.

Research method

- This was a laboratory experiment.
- The independent variables were:
  - the materials used/task given (number, mass, volume);
  - the children's age;
  - the experimental condition (standard Piagetian condition/one-judgement condition/fixed-array (control) condition).
- The dependent variable was the performance on the conservation tasks, measured by whether the participant was able to conserve number/mass/ volume.
- This study used an independent groups design. Each of the four age groups was subdivided into three experimental/task groups, and although each child was tested four times on each of the three materials (number, mass, volume), they only participated in one of the experimental conditions.

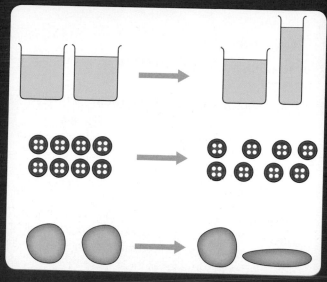

▲ **Figure 4.1** Samuel and Bryant's conservation tasks

- Rose and Blank's study was limited, however: it dealt only with the conservation of number and involved only one age group, 6-year-olds.
- This study built on previous research and aimed to find out whether younger and older children are affected in the same way by being asked a post-transformation question only once, and also whether other conservation tasks produce similar results.

Outline of the procedure/study

- Two hundred and fifty-two boys and girls, aged between 5 and 8.5 years, were drawn from schools and playgroups in and around Crediton, Devon.
- The children were divided into four age groups, whose mean ages were: 5 years, 3 months; 6 years, 3 months; 7 years, 3 months; 8 years, 3 months.
- Each age group was subdivided into three experimental conditions:
  - **Standard condition**: where the same question was asked both before and after witnessing the transformation.
  - **One-judgement condition**: where only one question was asked, after witnessing the transformation.
  - **Fixed-array (control) condition**: where one question was asked and the child did not see the transformation.
- Three kinds of materials were used in each experimental task condition:
  - Play-Doh to test for the conservation of mass.
  - Counters to test for the conservation of number.
  - Liquid to test for the conservation of volume.
- Each child was tested individually and was given four trials with each kind of material, two with equal and two with unequal quantities. The order of the trials and the order in which the three types of materials were presented were systematically varied between the children.

Key findings

▼ **Table 4.1** Mean errors out of 12 conservation tests (4 x 3 materials)

Age	Standard	One judgement	Fixed array
5	8.5	7.3	8.6
6	5.7	4.3	6.4
7	3.2	2.6	4.9
8	1.7	1.3	3.3

- Children were significantly more able to conserve in the one-judgement condition, supporting previous findings by Rose and Blank, and demonstrating the reliability of their results. This was true for all three types of material and for all four age groups.
- The older groups performed consistently better than the younger groups.
- The standard condition was found to be significantly easier than the fixed array.

▼ **Table 4.2** Mean errors (out of 4) in each condition

Material	Standard	One judgement	Fixed array
Mass	1.5	1.2	1.7
Number	1.5	1.0	1.5
Volume	1.8	1.6	2.5

The number task was found to be significantly easier than the mass or volume tasks.

Conclusions

- The ability to conserve improves with age. This supports Piaget's theory of cognitive development.
- Children can conserve at a younger age than that proposed by Piaget.
- Children who fail the traditional conservation task often understand the principle of invariance and make mistakes for extraneous reasons – for example, being asked the same question twice by an acknowledged authority figure. This supports Rose and Blank's criticism of Piaget's methodology.
- Conservation skills develop in stages, with the ability to conserve number developing before the ability to conserve mass or volume. This supports Piaget's notion of decalage.

Usefulness

- Piaget's theory has been widely used in education, as the theory suggests that children should only be taught or do things when they show cognitive preparedness. This study gives support for this notion in relation to conservation abilities, and reinforces the need for appropriate individualised learning programmes for children of all ages.
- This study shows that children may have developed certain cognitive abilities, but may not display them if not questioned appropriately. An acknowledged authority figure repeating the same question may influence children to change their answers against their better judgement. Teachers/role models should therefore ensure that they question children appropriately to increase the likelihood of getting a valid response.

Issues to be considered

- Strengths/weaknesses of laboratory experiments.
- Strengths/weaknesses of an independent measures design.
- Strengths/weaknesses of snapshot studies.
- Strengths/weaknesses of the sample.
- Strengths/weaknesses of quantitative data.
- Reliability.
- Validity and ecological validity.
- Ethics.

Exam tips for this study
- Know the research method, design and sample.
- Know the three experimental conditions.
- Know how the ability to conserve mass, number and volume was tested.
- Know the key findings.
- Be able to draw conclusions from the findings.
- Be able to suggest at least one way in which the study could be improved, and possible implications of the suggestion(s) for methodology, ethics, reliability, validity, usefulness, practicality, and so on.

Exam-style questions linked to this study

Section A

1 (a) Identify **two** features of the sample. **[2]**

   (b) Suggest **one** strength of this sample. **[2]**

2 (a) One of the experimental conditions was the standard condition. Identify the other **two** experimental conditions. **[2]**

   (b) Outline the standard condition. **[2]**

3 Describe how the children's ability to conserve number was tested. **[4]**

4 Explain why this study is considered a laboratory experiment. **[4]**

5 Suggest **two** conclusions that can be drawn from this study. **[4]**

6 Describe **two** ethical issues that could be raised in relation to this study. **[4]**

Section B

(a) Outline why this study was conducted. **[2]**

(b) Describe why this study is considered a snapshot study. **[4]**

(c) Referring to this study, suggest **one** strength and **one** weakness of snapshot studies. **[6]**

(d) Outline how children's ability to conserve number, mass and volume was tested in this study. **[8]**

(e) Suggest ways in which this study could be improved. **[8]**

(f) Discuss the issue of validity in relation to this study. **[8]**

Section C

(a) Outline the developmental approach. **[2]**

(b) With reference to this study, describe how the developmental approach could explain why one child can conserve while another cannot.

(c) Describe **one** similarity and **one** difference between any studies that take the developmental approach.

(d) Discuss strengths **and** weaknesses of the developmental approach, using any studies that take this approach. **[12]**

pp. 6, 528–35

31

BANDURA, ROSS AND ROSS (1961): IMITATING AGGRESSION

Transmission of aggression through imitation of aggressive models

▲ **Figure 4.2** A Bobo doll

Background to the study

- Previous research has shown that children will readily imitate behaviour demonstrated by an adult model if the model remains present (Bandura and Hudson, 1961).

- However, although such research has provided convincing evidence for the influence and control exerted by role models on the behaviour of others, until this study, little was known about how the behaviour displayed by a model might affect an individual in novel settings when the model is absent.

- Therefore, this study first exposed children to aggressive and non-aggressive adult models, and then tested the amount of imitative learning demonstrated by the children in a new situation in the absence of the model.

Relation to the developmental approach

- This approach is concerned with the study of psychological changes that occur throughout a person's lifespan. There are many changes that interest psychologists – for example, cognitive processes, such as thinking and problem-solving, social processes, such as developing relationships and the acquisition of moral understanding.

- Bandura, Ross and Ross's study focuses on the social process of how children learn about behaving aggressively. The study therefore links with the development of moral understanding and behaviour.

- Bandura, Ross and Ross argue that children develop views of the world through a process known as social learning, so, as children grow, they learn to be aggressive through this process.

Theory/ies on which the study is based

Social Learning Theory (SLT)

- SLT explains human behaviour in terms of a continuous interaction between cognitive, behavioural and environmental influences.

- According to SLT, aggressive behaviours are learned through reinforcement and the imitation of aggressive 'models' (Bandura, 1965, 1973, 1974).

- Imitation is the reproduction of learning through observation (observational learning), and involves observing other people who serve as models for behaviour.

- Bandura *et al.* (1961, 1963) showed how a child's aggressive tendencies can be strengthened through vicarious reinforcement (seeing others being rewarded for behaving aggressively – that is, not being punished).

Research method

- This was a laboratory experiment that used an independent measures, matched participants design.
- The independent variables were:
  - Whether the child witnessed an aggressive or a non-aggressive adult model in the first phase of the experiment (a control group was not exposed to an adult model).
  - The sex of the model (male or female).
  - The sex of the child (boy or girl).
- The dependent variable was the amount of imitative behaviour and aggression shown by the child in phase three, measured by the male model and, at times, a second researcher, observing each child through a one-way mirror and noting down at 5-second intervals: displays of imitative aggressive responses, partially imitative aggressive responses and/or non-aggressive imitative responses.
- The 72 children (36 boys, 36 girls), aged 37–69 months (mean 52 months), from Stanford University Nursery School, were matched through a procedure that pre-rated them for aggressiveness.
- Each child only participated in one of the experimental conditions – that is, boy + male aggressive/non-aggressive model; girl + male aggressive/non-aggressive model; boy + female aggressive/non-aggressive model; girl + female aggressive/non-aggressive model; control group (no model).

- The aim was to demonstrate that learning can occur through mere observation of a model, and that imitation of learned behaviour can occur in the absence of that model.
- There were four hypotheses:
  - Children shown aggressive models will show significantly more imitative aggressive acts resembling those of their models than those shown non-aggressive models or no models.
  - Children shown non-aggressive, subdued models will show significantly less aggressive behaviour than those shown aggressive models or no models.
  - Boys will show significantly more imitative aggression than girls.
  - Children will imitate same-sex model behaviour to a greater degree than opposite-sex behaviour.

Outline of the procedure/study

Phase 1

- Children in the experimental conditions were taken into a room individually and seated at a table to play with potato prints and picture stickers for 10 minutes, while:
  - The aggressive model began by assembling a tinker toy set, but after about a minute turned to a Bobo doll and spent the remainder of the period physically and verbally aggressing it, using a standardised procedure.
  - The non-aggressive model assembled the tinker toys in a quiet, subdued manner, totally ignoring the Bobo doll.
  - The control group did not participate in Phase 1.

Phase 2

- All the children were then taken to an anteroom individually and subjected to mild aggression arousal. Initially they were allowed to play with some very attractive toys, but after about 2 minutes the experimenter took the toys away, saying they were reserved for other children. However, they could play with any of the toys in the next room.

Phase 3

- Children were then taken individually into a third room, which contained both aggressive and non-aggressive toys – for example, a 3-foot-high Bobo doll, a mallet, dart guns, a tea set, cars, dolls. They were observed through a one-way mirror for 20 minutes, while observers recorded behaviour (with inter-scorer reliabilities of .90 product-moment coefficients) in the following categories:
  - imitative aggression (physical, verbal and non-aggressive speech)
  - partially imitative aggression
  - non-imitative physical and verbal aggression
  - non-aggressive behaviour.

Key findings

- Children in the aggressive condition showed significantly more imitation of physical and verbal aggressive behaviour and non-aggressive verbal responses than children in the non-aggressive or control conditions.

- Children in the aggressive condition showed more partial imitation and non-imitative physical and verbal aggression than those in the non-aggressive or control conditions. Results here, however, were not always significant.

- Children in the non-aggressive condition showed very little aggression, although results were not always significantly less than the control group.

- Children who saw the same-sex model imitated the model's behaviour significantly more in the following categories:

  - Boys imitated male models more than girls for physical and verbal aggression, non-imitative aggression and gun play.
  - Girls imitated female models more than boys for verbal imitative aggression and non-imitative aggression. However, results were not significant.

- The behaviour of the male model exerted greater influence than the female model.

- Overall, boys produced more imitative physical aggression than girls.

Conclusions

- Children will imitate aggressive/non-aggressive behaviours displayed by adult models, even if the model is not present.

- Children can learn behaviour though observation and imitation.

- Behaviour modelled by male adults has a greater influence on children's behaviour than behaviour modelled by female adults.

- Both boys and girls are more likely to learn highly masculine-typed behaviour, such as physical aggression, from a male adult than from a female adult.

- Boys and girls are likely to learn verbal aggression from a same-sex adult.

Usefulness

- This study shows that children can learn and reproduce behaviour modelled by significant others. Therefore, as a society, we can determine what behaviours are to be considered acceptable for adults to model in front of children. In Western society, aggression towards others is generally considered unacceptable, and should therefore not be modelled by role models. Other societies, however, consider aggression acceptable and encourage adults to model aggressive behaviour.

- This study indicates that children can learn both antisocial and prosocial behaviours from various sources within their immediate environment, such as the media. Controls can therefore be placed on media sources in relation to the types of behaviour children can be exposed to – for example, the 9.00pm watershed on TV, and film and video age ratings to reduce exposure to antisocial behaviours. Likewise, prosocial behaviours can be displayed to encourage children to behave in socially acceptable ways.

Issues to be considered

- Strengths/weaknesses of laboratory experiments.
- Strengths/weaknesses of an independent measures design.
- Strengths/weaknesses of snapshot studies.
- Strengths/weaknesses of observation as a way to gather data.
- Strengths/weaknesses of quantitative and qualitative data.
- Strengths/weaknesses of the sample.
- Reliability.
- Validity and ecological validity.
- Ethics.

▲ **Figure 4.3** Stills from Bandura, Ross and Ross's study, where children mimic an adult's (top row) aggression towards a Bobo doll

Exam tips for this study

● Know the research method and sample.
● Know the experimental and control conditions.
● Know the procedure.
● Know the key findings.
● Be able to draw conclusions from the findings.
● Be able to suggest at least one way in which the study could be improved, and possible implications of the suggestion(s) for methodology, ethics, reliability, validity, usefulness, practicality, and so on.

Exam-style questions linked to this study

Section A

1 Describe the research method used in this study. **[4]**
2 Describe the sample used in this study. **[4]**
3 **(a)** Describe how participants were matched in this study **[2]**
  (b) Explain why participants were matched in this study. **[2]**
4 Describe how the model's behaviour was manipulated in this study. **[4]**
5 **(a)** Outline how the participants were subjected to mild aggression arousal. **[2]**
  (b) Explain why participants were subjected to mild aggression arousal. **[2]**
6 Outline **two** conclusions that can be drawn from this study. **[4]**

Section B

(a) Describe **one** theory on which this study was based. **[4]**
(b) Outline how observation was used to gather data in this study. **[4]**
(c) Suggest **one** strength of how observation was used to gather data in this study. **[4]**
(d) Outline the key findings of this study. **[8]**
(e) Discuss the issue of ecological validity in relation to this study. **[8]**
(f) Suggest ways in which the ecological validity of this study could be improved. **[8]**

Section C

(a) Describe **one** implication of the developmental approach. **[2]**
(b) With reference to this study, describe how the developmental approach could explain aggression. **[4]**
(c) Describe **one** similarity and **one** difference between any of the core studies that take the developmental approach.
(d) Discuss strengths **and** weaknesses of the developmental approach, using examples from any of the core studies that take this approach.

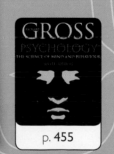

GROSS
PSYCHOLOGY
THE SCIENCE OF MIND AND BEHAVIOUR

p. 455

FREUD (1909): LITTLE HANS
Analysis of a phobia of a five-year old boy

Background to the study

- Hans was described as a cheerful and straightforward child, but when he became 'ill' (developed his phobia) it was obvious that there was a difference between what he said and what he thought. Freud thought this was because things were going on in Hans's unconscious mind of which he was unaware.

- Freud therefore decided to help Hans by interpreting his behaviour and telling him why he was thinking and behaving as he was. This is a process known as psychoanalysis.

Relation to the developmental approach

- The developmental approach assumes that there are clearly identifiable, systematic changes that influence an individual's behaviour from conception to death.

- It is generally acknowledged that childhood experiences play an important role in shaping who we become as adults, and that the development of behaviour is an interaction between nature and nurture.

- Freud's explanation for Hans's unusual behaviour relates directly to his theory of psychosexual development. The first trait relating to this theory was when Hans started to show a 'lively interest in his widdler' (Freud, 1909), indicating that he had entered the phallic stage of development. His subsequent development of a fear of horses was a clear indication that Hans was experiencing the Oedipus complex, and so was still in the phallic stage. By the end of the study, Hans was 5 years old and Freud interpreted his fantasies about a plumber to mean he was now identifying with his father, so had overcome the Oedipus complex and come to the end of the phallic stage.

Theory/ies on which the study is based

Theory of infantile sexuality/Theory of psychosexual development

- According to Freud's theory, sexuality is not confined to physically mature adults, but is evident from birth. However, different parts of the body are particularly sensitive at different times during childhood.

- The sequence of the psychosexual stages are determined by maturation (nature) and how the child is treated by others (nurture).

- Freud's stages of psychosexual development are usually considered to be: (1) oral stage: 0–1 year; anal stage: 1–3 years; phallic stage: 3–5/6 years; latency stage: 5/6 years to puberty; genital stage: puberty to maturity.

- The Oedipus complex for boys and the Electra complex for girls form part of the phallic stage.

Research method

- This, like the Thigpen and Cleckley study, was a longitudinal case study.
- A case study gathers detailed data of either a single individual or a very small group of individuals, an institution or an event. Here, in-depth, detailed data were gathered on one individual – Little Hans – in relation to his fantasies, fears and phobias.
- The study is considered longitudinal as it documents developments in Hans's fears, from when he was 3 years old until he was 5. This allowed Freud to link the evidence gathered to his developmental theory of sexuality.
- Data were gathered by Little Hans's father (a firm believer of Freud's ideas), regularly observing and questioning Hans. He then sent records of the events and conversations to Freud, who interpreted the information and replied to Little Hans's father with advice on how to proceed.

- Freud therefore documented the case of Little Hans, to show how his fears, dreams and fantasies were symbolic of his unconscious passing through the phallic stage of psychosexual development.
- Freud used this study to support his ideas about the origins of phobias, his theory of infantile sexuality and the Oedipus complex, and his belief in the effectiveness of psychoanalytic therapy.

Outline of the procedure/study

- Just before he was 3 years old, Hans started to show a lively interest in his 'widdler', and the presence/absence of this organ in others – human and non-human.
- At this time he had a tendency to masturbate, bringing threats from his mother to send for Dr A. to cut it off.
- When he was 3½ years old, Hans gained a baby sister, Hanna, whom he resented and, subsequently, subconsciously, wished his mother would drop in the bath so she would drown.
- Later Hans developed a fear of being bitten by white horses. This seemed to be linked to two incidents:
  - overhearing a father say to a child, 'Don't put your finger to the white horse or it will bite you';
  - seeing a horse that was pulling a carriage fall down and kick about with its legs.

His fear was then generalised to carts and buses.

- Both before and after the development of the phobias (of the bath and horses), Hans was anxious that his mother would go away, and was prone to fantasies and daydreams. These included:
  - the giraffe fantasy;
  - two plumber fantasies;
  - the parenting fantasy.
- Having received 'help' from his father and Freud, after the parenting fantasy, both the 'illness' and analysis came to an end.

▲ **Figure 4.4**

Key findings

- Little Hans's fear of horses was considered by Freud to be a subconscious fear of his father. This was because the dark around the mouth of a horse plus the blinkers resembled the moustache and glasses worn by his father. He was fearful of his father because he was experiencing the Oedipus complex.

- Hans's fascination with his 'widdler' was because he was experiencing the Oedipus complex.

- Hans's daydream about giraffes was a representation of him trying to take his mother away from his father, so he could have her to himself – another feature of the Oedipus complex.

- Hans's fantasy of becoming a father again linked to him experiencing the Oedipus complex.

- Hans's fantasy about the plumber was interpreted as him now identifying with his father and having passed through the Oedipus complex.

Usefulness

- Little Hans was the only child studied by Freud, and his fear of horses may have been caused by a traumatic event that had nothing to do with his father. Freud had already formulated his theories relating to infantile sexuality and the Oedipus complex before he studied Hans, so his form of questioning may have been biased. These are just two reasons why the validity of this study is questionable.

- There are other, equally plausible explanations for Hans's phobia – for example, Fromm (castration anxiety from the mother), Bowlby (attachment theory), learning theory (classical conditioning of phobias).

- Even so, few people question the major contribution that Freud made to the understanding of behaviour and the role played by the unconscious mind in influencing the way individuals behave. The fact that psychoanalysis is still widely used today shows the usefulness of Freud's work.

Conclusions

- Freud concluded that his study of Hans provided support for:
  - his theory of psychosexual development/infant sexuality;
  - his suggestion that boys in the phallic stage of psychosexual development experience the Oedipus complex;
  - the nature of phobias, and his theory that they are the product of unconscious anxiety displaced onto harmless external objects;
  - his concept of unconscious determinism, which holds that people are not consciously aware of the causes of their behaviour
  - his use of psychoanalytic therapy to treat disturbed thoughts, feelings and behaviours, by first identifying the unconscious cause(s) of the disturbance and then bringing this into the conscious, so that it can be discussed and resolved.

Issues to be considered

- Strengths/weaknesses of case studies.
- Strengths/weaknesses of longitudinal studies.
- Strengths/weaknesses of self-reports as a way to gather data.
- Strengths/weaknesses of observations as a way to gather data.
- Strengths/weaknesses of the sample.
- Strengths/weaknesses of qualitative data.
- Reliability.
- Validity and ecological validity.
- Ethics.

Exam-style questions linked to this study

Section A

1 Outline the Oedipus complex. **[4]**
2 **(a)** Identify **two** of Hans's phobias. **[2]**
   (b) Describe **one** of Hans' phobias. **[2]**
3 Describe **one** of Hans's fantasies or daydreams. **[4]**
4 **(a)** Outline how data were gathered in this study. **[2]**
   (b) Outline **one** limitation of the way data were gathered in this study. **[2]**
5 Describe **two** pieces of qualitative data gathered in this study. **[4]**
6 Describe **two** ethical issues that could be raised in relation to this study. **[4]**

Section B

(a) Outline the aims of this study. **[4]**
(b) Describe why this study is considered a longitudinal case study. **[4]**
(c) Describe **one** strength and **one** weakness of longitudinal studies as used here by Freud. **[6]**
(d) Describe **three** key findings from this study. **[6]**
(e) Briefly discuss the issue of validity in relation to this study. **[6]**
(f) Suggest how this study could be improved **and** consider the implications of your suggestions. **[10]**

Section C

(a) Describe **one** assumption of the developmental approach. **[2]**
(b) Referring to this study, describe how the developmental approach might explain phobias. **[4]**
(c) Describe **one** similarity and **one** difference between this study and any other study that can take the developmental approach. **[6]**
(d) Discuss strengths **and** weaknesses of the developmental approach, supporting your answer with examples from this study. **[12]**

Exam tips for this study

- Know Freud's psychosexual stages of development.
- Be able to describe the Oedipus complex.
- Know the research method and how data were gathered.
- Be able to describe at least two of Hans's fantasies and two of Hans's phobias.
- Know the key findings, as explained by Freud.
- Be able to draw conclusions from the findings.
- Be able to suggest at least one way in which the study could be improved, and possible implications of the suggestion(s) for methodology, ethics, reliability, validity, usefulness, practicality, and so on.

▲ Figure 4.5

GROSS
PSYCHOLOGY
THE SCIENCE OF MIND AND BEHAVIOUR

pp. 548–9, 730–2

MAGUIRE *ET AL.* (2000): TAXI DRIVERS' BRAINS

Navigation related structural changes in the hippocampi of taxi drivers

Background to the study

- Research has shown increased hippocampal volume relative to brain and body size in small mammals and birds that show behaviour requiring spatial memory (e.g. food storing).
- In some species, hippocampal volumes enlarge during seasons when spatial ability is greatest.
- Research has also shown that there are differences in the structure of healthy human brains – for example, between males and females, musicians and non-musicians.
- However past research has not shown:
  - whether differences in brain structure are susceptible to plastic change in response to environmental stimulation;
  - the precise role of the hippocampus in humans;

Relation to the physiological approach

- The physiological approach attempts to explain behaviour through an understanding of biological and neurological processes.
- The physiological workings of the body and brain therefore determine how an individual behaves.
- Maguire et al. hypothesised that experiences can cause changes in the brain, and discovered that people who constantly use navigational skills in their work show differences in the part of the brain (hippocampus) that deals with these skills when compared to those who do not constantly use such skills – for example, London taxi drivers have a significantly greater posterior hippocampal volume than non-taxi drivers.

Theory/ies on which the study is based

- The hippocampus is one of the major structures of the limbic system. The human limbic system is very similar to that of primitive animals and is often referred to as the 'old mammalian brain'. It is closely involved with behaviours that satisfy certain motivational, learning and emotional needs, including feeding, fighting, escape and mating.
- The hippocampus plays an important role in the laying down of new memories. It is found inside each hemisphere of the brain and is thought to play an important role in facilitating spatial memory and navigation. Recent research, such as this study, has indicated that lesions to the hippocampus affect an individual's ability to remember the location of different places and things.

Research method

- This was a quasi/natural experiment because the independent variable – whether the participant was a London taxi driver or a person who did not drive taxis – was naturally varying, so could not be manipulated or controlled by the researchers. The dependent variable was the volume of the hippocampi, including their anterior, body and posterior regions, measured by analysing MRI scans of participants' brains, using the two techniques of VBM (voxel-based morphometry) and pixel counting.
- The study used an independent measures, matched participants design.
- The sample of 16 taxi drivers were all healthy, right-handed, male London taxi drivers, with a mean age of 44 years (range 32–62 years), and mean time as a licensed London taxi driver (passed 'The Knowledge') 14.3 years (range 1.5–42 years). The control group who did not drive taxis (50 for the VBM analysis, 16 for the pixel counting) were matched for health, handedness, sex, mean age and age range.

- whether the human brain responds to experiences requiring spatial memory in the same way as the brains of smaller mammals and birds.

- Maguire therefore aimed to show that the hippocampus in the human brain is the structure associated with spatial memory and navigation.

- Her sample of London taxi drivers was ideal, because they have to acquire extensive spatial and navigational information (pass 'The Knowledge') on the city of London to gain their taxi driving licence.

- Her use of a group of taxi drivers with a wide range of navigational experience allowed her to examine the direct effect of spatial experience on brain structure.

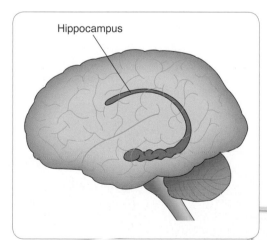

▲ Figure 5.1 The hippocampus

Outline of the procedure/study

- The scans of the control group were selected from the structural MRI scan database at the same unit where the taxi drivers were scanned.
- The MRI scans of all participants were analysed using:

  - VBM, which is an automatic procedure that 'normalises' the scans to a template to eliminate overall brain size as a variable, and then identifies differences in grey matter density in different regions of the brain. The brains of the 16 taxi drivers were compared to those of 50 non-taxi drivers to see if there were any differences in structure.

  - pixel counting, which compared the volume of anterior, body and posterior cross-sections of the taxi drivers' hippocampi with a sample of 16 controls, taken from the 50 used in the VBM analysis, who had already been matched for age, gender and handedness. The images were analysed by one person experienced in the technique and blinded to whether the scan was of a taxi driver or a control, and to the VBM findings. This procedure allowed the total hippocampal volume to be calculated.

Key findings

- VBM analysis showed no significant differences between the brains of the two groups, except:
  - taxi drivers had significantly increased grey matter volume in the right and left posterior hippocampi compared to controls;
  - in the controls there was a relatively greater grey matter volume in the anterior hippocampi compared to taxi drivers.
- Pixel counting showed that although there was no significant difference in overall volume of the hippocampi between the two groups:
  - taxi drivers had a significantly greater posterior hippocampal volume than controls;
  - controls had a significantly greater anterior right hippocampal volume than the taxi drivers, and a significantly greater hippocampal body volume on the right than the left.

▼ **Table 5.1** Regions of the brain with the largest volume

	Left hippocampus	Right hippocampus
Anterior		CONTROLS
Body		CONTROLS
Posterior	TAXI DRIVERS	TAXI DRIVERS

- Correlations showed a significant positive correlation between the length of time as a taxi driver and the right posterior hippocampal volume, but a negative correlation for the anterior hippocampal volume.

Conclusions

- There are regionally specific structural differences between the hippocampi of licensed London taxi drivers compared to those who do not drive London taxis.
- The professional dependence on navigational skills in licensed London taxi drivers is associated with a relative redistribution of grey matter in the hippocampus.
- It can be suggested that the changes in the arrangement of hippocampal grey matter are acquired – that is, due to nurture.
- Findings also indicate the possibility of local plasticity in the structure of a normal human brain, which allows it to adapt in response to prolonged environmental stimuli.

Usefulness

- The demonstration that normal activities (driving a London taxi) can induce changes in the relative volume of grey matter in areas of the brain has great implications for rehabilitating individuals who have suffered brain injury or disease. If specific demands can be made on the brain, it may be able to respond by using grey matter from areas of the brain not damaged, thus enabling the individual to overcome problems caused by injury or disease.
- One must remember that this study:
  - only looked at changes in hippocampal volume – other regions of the brain may not have the ability to adapt to environmental stimuli;
  - does not show how brain changes occur.

Issues to be considered

- Strengths/weaknesses of quasi/natural experiments.
- Strengths/weaknesses of the independent measures design.
- Strengths/weaknesses of correlations.
- Strengths/weaknesses of snapshot studies.
- Strengths/weaknesses of quantitative data.
- Strengths/weaknesses of the sample.
- Reliability.
- Validity and ecological validity.
- Ethics.

Exam tips for this study
- Know the research method and sample.
- Know how the MRI scans were analysed, and be able to describe VBM and pixel counting.
- Know the key findings.
- Be able to draw conclusions from the findings.
- Be able to suggest at least one way in which the study could be improved, and possible implications of the suggestion(s) for methodology, ethics, reliability, validity, usefulness, practicality, and so on.

Exam-style questions linked to this study

Section A

1 Explain why this study is considered a quasi/natural experiment. **[4]**
2 Describe the sample used in this study. **[4]**
3 Describe 'The Knowledge'. **[4]**
4 **(a)** Identify the **two** techniques used to analyse the MRI scans. **[2]**
  (b) Outline **one** of the techniques used to analyse the MRI scans. **[2]**
5 Describe **two** controls used in this study. **[4]**
6 Outline **two** findings from this study. **[4]**

Section B

(a) Outline the aim of this study. **[2]**
(b) Describe the sample used and give **one** limitation of the sample. **[6]**
(c) Describe the procedure used in this study. **[6]**
(d) Briefly discuss the issue of reliability in relation to this study. **[6]**
(e) Outline the key findings of this study. **[8]**
(f) Suggest **two** ways in which this study could be improved. **[8]**

Section C

(a) Outline the physiological approach. **[2]**
(b) Referring to this study, describe how the physiological approach can explain structural changes in the brain. **[4]**
(c) Describe **one** similarity and **one** difference between this study and any other core study that takes the physiological approach.
(d) Discuss strengths **and** weaknesses of the physiological approach, using examples from any of the core studies that take this approach **[12]**

GROSS
PSYCHOLOGY
THE SCIENCE OF MIND AND BEHAVIOUR
SIXTH EDITION

p. **60**

DEMENT AND KLEITMAN (1957): REM SLEEP AND DREAMING

The relation of eye movements during sleep to dream activity, an objective method for the study of dreaming

Background to the study

- Three measures are usually taken to describe the sleep stages:
  - gross brainwave activity/electrical activity in the brain, measured by an electroencephalogram (EEG);
  - electrical activity of a muscle, measured by an electromyogram (EMG);
  - eye movement, measured by an electro-oculogram (EOG).

- A relationship between dream activity and physiological variables was reported by Aserinsky and Kleitman (1955), who observed periods of rapid, conjugate eye movements during sleep and found these were associated with a high incidence of dream recall.

Relation to the physiological approach

- During a normal night's sleep, an individual will pass through a series of physiologically controlled sleep cycles. Each cycle has four stages, through which one moves downwards and upwards continuously while asleep. After the first cycle of sleep has been completed, the first stage becomes known as 'active sleep', a characteristic of which is rapid eye movement (REM).

- A feature of REM sleep is the appearance of pontine-geniculo-occipital (PGO) spikes/waves. Epsom (1993) found PGO activity to be the prime source of dreaming.

- This study showed that when participants were woken from the physiologically induced state of REM sleep/PGO activity, they reported they had been dreaming and that there was a relationship between their patterns of eye movements in REM sleep and dream content.

Theory/ies on which the study is based

- Sleep is a specialised state that has evolved in all animals to serve particular functions.
- In humans, a typical night's sleep comprises a number of ultradian cycles (lasting approximately 90 minutes), each containing a number of stages:
  - stage 1: the 'drifting' stage, passed through on the way to deep sleep;
  - stage 2: a deeper stage from which one can still be easily woken;
  - stage 3: sleep becomes deeper and waking is difficult;
  - stage 4: deep or quiet sleep.
- During each sleep cycle an individual moves 'down' through all four stages and then moves up again, but instead of re-entering stage 1, a different kind of sleep (active sleep) appears.
- This active sleep is known as rapid eye movement sleep (REM sleep).
- As the night progresses, an individual spends more time in REM than non-REM (NREM) sleep (stages 2–4).

Research method

- This study can be considered as either a laboratory experiment or a quasi/natural experiment.
- The fact that the researcher controlled when participants woke up makes it a laboratory experiment.
- However, because the independent variable (REM/NREM) could not be manipulated by the researcher, as it occurred naturally, the study can also be considered a quasi/natural experiment.
- The dependent variable was the recall of dreams.
- Correlation was also used to analyse the relationship between patterns of REM and dream content.

- This study aimed to provide a more detailed investigation of how objective, physiological aspects of REM relate to the subjective experience of dreaming, by testing whether:
  - significantly more dreaming occurs during REM than NREM sleep (Study 1);
  - there is a significant positive correlation between objective time spent in REM and subjective duration of dreaming (Study 2);
  - there is a significant relationship between the pattern of eye movements during sleep and dream content (Study 3).

Outline of the procedure/study

- Seven adult males and two adult females made up the sample. Five were studied intensively, while data from the other four were used to confirm findings.
- Participants reported to the laboratory just before their normal bedtime. They had been instructed to eat normally, but to abstain from alcoholic or caffeinated drinks on the days of the experiment. Electrodes were attached near the eyes to measure eye movement (EOG), and on the scalp to measure brainwave frequency as a criterion of depth of sleep (EEG). Participants then went to bed in a quiet, darkened room. At various times during the night, they were woken up by a doorbell placed near the bed and instructed to state whether or not they had been dreaming, and, if they had, the content of the dream. There was no contact between the experimenter and the participant until the participant had finished speaking. Then, occasionally, the experimenter would enter the room to question the participant on some particular point of the dream.
- To compare whether they had been dreaming, participants were woken either during REM or NREM sleep.
- To assess if participants could judge how long they had been dreaming, they were woken either 5 or 15 minutes after the onset of REM.
- The length of dream (measured by the number of words in the dream narrative) was correlated to the duration of REM sleep before awakening.
- To study the relationship between patterns of REM and dream content, participants were woken after 1 minute of vertical/horizontal/vertical + horizontal/very little or no eye movement and asked to describe their dream.

Key findings

- All participants had REM activity every night.
- REM periods occurred at regular intervals and were specific to each individual.
- The average for the whole group was one REM period every 92 minutes.
- REM periods tended to last longer as the night progressed.

Study 1

- Significantly more dreams were reported in REM than NREM: 152 compared to 11.
- There were individual differences – for example, participant KC recalled dreams after REM awakenings 36/40 times, compared to 26/34 by participant DN.
- Failure to recall dreams usually occurred early in the night.
- Dream recall from NREM tended to occur when participants were woken within 8 minutes after the end of an REM period.

Study 2

- Many of the participants were very accurate in their estimations of dream length – 45/51 estimates were correct for the awakenings 5 minutes into REM, and 47/60 estimates were correct for the awakenings 15 minutes into REM.
- There was a significant positive correlation between length of dream narrative and duration of REM before awakening.

Study 3

- There was a strong association between pattern of eye movements and dream content – for example, horizontal REM: a dream of watching two people throw tomatoes at each other; vertical REM: a dream of climbing up a series of ladders, looking up and down while climbing.

Conclusions

- Dreaming is accompanied by REM activity.
- It cannot be stated with complete certainty that dream activity does not occur in other sleep stages.
- Regular periods of REM and dreaming are an intrinsic part of normal sleep.
- Dreams can be studied in an objective way.

Usefulness

- Because an objective measurement of dreaming can be obtained by recording REMs during sleep, it is possible to objectively study the effect on dreaming of environmental changes, psychological stress, drug administration, and a variety of other factors and influences.
- Research such as this has encouraged further research into sleep and dreaming. Sleep laboratories are now widespread, and much more is now known about things like sleep deprivation, sleepwalking, sleep problems and the effects of environmental stimuli (e.g. music, noise, temperature) on sleep patterns. Unfortunately, to date, little is really known about dreaming per se.

Issues to be considered

- Strengths/weaknesses of the research method.
- Strengths/weaknesses of objective measures of behaviour.
- Strengths/weaknesses of the sample.
- Strengths/weaknesses of quantitative and qualitative data.
- Strengths/weaknesses of correlations.
- Reliability.
- Validity and ecological validity.
- Ethics.

Exam-style questions linked to this study

Section A

1 (a) Identify **two** features of the sample. **[2]**

(b) Describe **one** limitation of the sample. **[2]**

2 Describe rapid eye movement sleep (REM). **[4]**

3 (a) Outline what an EEG measures. **[2]**

(b) Describe **one** limitation of using an EEG to investigate dreaming. **[2]**

4 Describe how the length of REM periods and subjective dreaming duration were measured. **[4]**

5 Describe **two** findings from the table below, showing the number of dreams recalled. **[4]**

▼ Table 5.2

Participant	REM sleep	NREM sleep
DN	17/26	3/24
IR	26/34	2/31
KC	36/40	3/34
WD	37/42	1/35
PM	24/30	2/25

6 Outline **two** ways in which this study lacks ecological validity. **[4]**

Section B

(a) Outline the aim of this study. **[2]**

(b) Describe how correlation was used to analyse data in this study. **[4]**

(c) Describe **one** strength and **one** weakness of correlations as used in this study. **[6]**

(d) Describe the procedure followed in this study. **[8]**

(e) Suggest how this study could be improved. **[8]**

(f) Consider the implications of the improvement(s) you have suggested. **[8]**

Section C

(a) Describe **one** assumption of the physiological approach. **[2]**

(b) Describe how the physiological approach might explain dreaming. **[4]**

(c) Describe **one** similarity and **one** difference between this and any other study that takes the physiological approach. **[6]**

(d) Discuss strengths **and** weaknesses of the physiological approach, using examples from Dement Kleitman's study to support your answer. **[12]**

Exam tips for this study

● Know the sample.

● Know how and why at least two controls were used in this study.

● Know the procedure and how both quantitative and qualitative data were gathered.

● Know the key findings for all three studies.

● Be able to draw conclusions from the findings.

● Be able to suggest at least one way in which the study could be improved, and possible implications of the suggestion(s) for methodology, ethics, reliability, validity, usefulness, practicality, and so on.

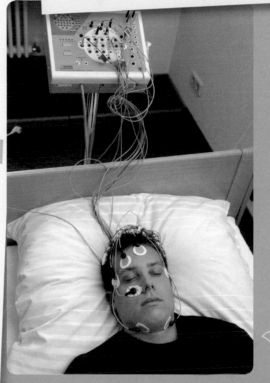

▲ **Figure 5.2** A sleep laboratory

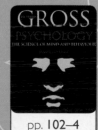

GROSS
PSYCHOLOGY
THE SCIENCE OF MIND AND BEHAVIOUR

pp. 102–4

SPERRY (1968): SPLIT BRAINS
Hemisphere deconnection and unity in conscious awareness

Relation to the physiological approach

- All that is psychological is first physiological – that is, since the mind appears to reside in the brain, all thoughts, feelings and behaviours ultimately have a physiological cause.

- The physiological approach could explain the difficulties experienced by individuals with a 'split-brain', because their brains work differently to those of 'normal' people. As a result of having their corpus callosum severed, the two hemispheres of the brain work independently and, unlike a 'normal' brain, do not transfer information from one side to the other. This inability to transfer information means that split-brain patients cannot do certain things a 'normal' person can.

- This was demonstrated in Sperry's study, which showed, for example, that if an object was presented to the left visual field, which was registered by the right hemisphere of split-brain patients, they were unable to name what they had seen. A 'normal' person would have no difficulty naming the object. This is because the language centre of the brain is in the left hemisphere, and in split-brain patients, information presented to the right hemisphere cannot be transferred to the left for identification through language.

Background to the study

- Previous research using split-brain animals showed numerous behavioural effects (Myers, 1961; Sperry, 1967a, 1976b).

- Other research by Sperry, on both humans and monkeys that had undergone surgical section of the corpus callosum, suggested the behavioural effects of this surgery may be less severe than other forms of cerebral surgery (e.g. frontal lobotomy).

- Research by Akelaitis (1944) also showed no important behavioural effects of surgical section of the corpus callosum in humans, provided other brain damage was excluded.

Theory/ies on which the study is based

- Although the right and left hemispheres are in many ways mirror images of each other, there are distinct areas dealing with speech production and comprehension (Broca's area and Wernike's area, respectively), showing their functional localisation. Functional lateralisation also exists, because Broca's and Wernike's areas are only found in the left hemisphere.

- The primary motor cortex is situated in the frontal lobe, and areas in the right hemisphere receive information from and are concerned with the activities of the left side of the body, and vice versa.

- Sperry believes that studies involving split-brain patients reveal the 'true' nature of the two hemispheres, because a commissurotomy, which deconnects the two hemispheres, means they can only work independently.

Research method

- This is usually considered a quasi/natural experiment, because the independent variable – having a split brain or not – was not directly manipulated by the researchers. Participants with split-brains had already undergone hemisphere deconnection to reduce severe epilepsy. No actual control group was necessary for comparison in the study, because the functions and abilities of the visual fields and hemispheres in non-split-brain individuals were already known.
- The dependent variable was the participants' ability to perform a variety of visual and tactile tests.
- It has been argued, however, that because such extensive tests were carried out on a very small sample (11 split-brain patients in total), this study can be considered a collection of case studies.

- More recent research by Sperry (1967b, 1976a) and Sperry *et al.* (1968), using appropriate tests, has actually shown a large number of behavioural effects that correlate directly with the loss of the neocortical commissures in man as well as animals.

- Sperry therefore set out in this study, using split-brain patients, to show that each hemisphere:
  - possesses an independent stream of conscious awareness;
  - has its own separate chain of memories that are inaccessible to the other hemisphere.

Outline of the procedure/study

Presenting visual information

- The participant, with one eye covered, centred the gaze on a fixed point in the centre of an upright translucent screen. Visual stimuli on 35-millimetre transparencies were arranged in a standard projector and were then back-projected at one-tenth of a second or less – too fast for eye movements to get the information into the wrong visual field. Everything projected to the left of the central meridian of the screen is passed via the left visual field (LVF) to the right hemisphere, and vice versa (regardless of which eye is used).

Presenting tactile information

- Below the translucent screen there was a gap, so that participants could reach objects, but not see their hands. Objects were then placed in either the participant's right/left or both hands. Information about objects placed in the left hand is processed by the right hemisphere, and vice versa.

▲ **Figure 5.3** A tachistocope

Participants undertook a variety of both visual and tactile tests. This apparatus called a tachistoscope.

Key findings

Visual tests

- Information shown and responded to in one visual field could only be recognised again if shown to the same visual field.

- Information presented to the RVF (LH system of a typical right-handed patient) could be described in speech and writing (with the right hand). If the same information is presented to the LVF (RH), participants insisted either that they did not see anything or that there was only a flash of light on the left side – that is, the information could not be described in speech or writing. However, participants could point with the left hand (RH) to a matching picture/object presented among a collection of pictures/objects.

- If different figures were presented simultaneously to different visual fields (e.g. $ sign to the LVF and ? to the RVF), participants could draw the $ sign with the left hand, but reported that they had seen ?.

Tactile tests

- Objects placed in the right hand (LH) could be described in speech or writing (with the right hand). If the same objects were placed in the left hand (RH), participants could only make wild guesses, and often seemed unaware that they were holding anything.

- Objects felt by one hand were only recognised again by the same hand – for example, objects first sensed by the right hand could not be retrieved by the left.

- When two objects were placed simultaneously in each hand and then hidden in a pile of objects, both hands selected their own object and ignored the other hand's object.

Conclusions

- People with split brains have two separate visual inner worlds, each with its own train of visual images.

- Split-brain patients have a lack of cross-integration, where a second hemisphere does not know what the first hemisphere has been doing.

- Split-brain patients seem to have two independent streams of consciousness, each with its own memories, perceptions and impulses – that is, two minds in one body.

Usefulness

- This research has useful implications for helping patients with brain damage. Before Sperry's research, little was known about the abilities of the right (minor) hemisphere. However, tests with split-brain patients showed that this hemisphere has a range of higher-order mental abilities, including some verbal comprehension, and is dominant in such abilities as spatial awareness and emotion.

- The study revealed the importance of the corpus callosum as a pathway for internal communication between the two sides of the brain, and behavioural limitations that may result from damage to this area of the brain.

Issues to be considered

- Strengths/weaknesses of laboratory experiments.
- Strengths/weaknesses of snapshot studies.
- Strengths/weaknesses of the sample.
- Strengths/weaknesses of quantitative data.
- Reliability.
- Validity and ecological validity.
- Ethics.

Exam-style questions linked to this study

Section A

1 **(a)** Outline the major function of the corpus callosum. **[2]**

(b) Outline why participants in this study had undergone a split-brain operation. **[2]**

2 Outline how visual stimuli were presented to the left visual field (LVF). **[4]**

3 Visual stimuli were presented to one visual field at a time. Outline **two** findings from these tests. **[4]**

4 Outline **two** findings from the tactile tests. **[4]**

5 Explain why split-brain patients do not usually notice that their mental functions have been cut in half. **[4]**

6 Sperry states that in split-brain patients, 'the left and right halves of the visual field seem to be perceived quite separately in each hemisphere with little or no cross-influence.' Describe **two** pieces of evidence that support this statement. **[4]**

Section B

(a) Outline why the sample was chosen. **[2]**

(b) Describe the research method used in this study. **[4]**

(c) Describe how qualitative data were gathered in this study. **[6]**

(d) With reference to this study, describe **one** strength and **one** weakness of qualitative data. **[6]**

(e) Outline some key findings of this study. **[8]**

(f) Suggest how this study could be improved, and consider the implications of your suggestions. **[10]**

Section C

(a) Describe **one** implication of the physiological approach. **[2]**

(b) With reference to this study, describe how the physiological approach could explain possible difficulties experienced by split-brain patients. **[4]**

(c) Describe **one** similarity and **one** difference between Sperry's study and any other studies that can take the physiological approach. **[6]**

(d) Discuss strengths **and** weaknesses of the physiological approach, using examples from any studies that take this approach. **[12]**

Exam tips for this study

- Know that:
  - RVF → LH → right hand
  - LVF → RH → left hand.
- Know the research method (for both visual and tactile tests) and the sample.
- Know the key findings.
- Be able to draw conclusions from the findings.
- Be able to suggest at least one way in which the study could be improved, and possible implications of the suggestion(s) for methodology, ethics, reliability, validity, usefulness, practicality, and so on.

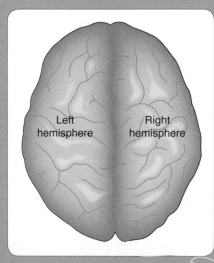

▲ **Figure 5.4** A split brain

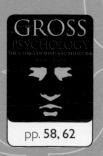

GROSS
PSYCHOLOGY
THE SCIENCE OF MIND AND BEHAVIOUR

pp. **58, 62**

MILGRAM (1963): OBEDIENCE
Behavioural study of obedience

Background to the study

● From 1939 to 1945, millions of innocent people were systematically slaughtered on command. Such inhumane actions may have originated in the mind of one person, but they could only have been carried out on such a massive scale because large numbers of people obeyed.

● History and observation suggest that for many people obedience is such an ingrained behavioural tendency that it will override training in ethics, empathy and moral values. This is because when given extreme commands by legitimate authority figures, subordinates adopt an agentic state, where they become the instrument for carrying out another person's wishes.

Relation to the social approach

● One assumption of the social approach is that other people and the surrounding environment are major influences on an individual's behaviour, thought processes and emotions.

● The social approach, as demonstrated through this study, could explain obedience. First, as Milgram himself suggested, the environment – Yale University – may have influenced participants with regard to the worthiness of the study and the competence of the experimenter, resulting in high levels of obedience that might not be found in a less prestigious setting. Second, the presence of what appeared to be a legitimate authority figure, dressed in a white lab coat, carrying a clipboard, may have influenced the participants' behaviour, as they believed him (through socialisation) to be a trustworthy and knowledgeable individual who should be obeyed.

Theory/ies on which the study is based

● Obedience is the psychological mechanism that links individual action to political purpose. It is the dispositional feature that binds people to systems of authority. It is an active or deliberate form of social influence.

● According to Milgram (1992), obedience involves the 'abdication of individual judgement in the face of some external social pressure'.

● Obedience involves (a) being ordered or instructed to do something; (b) being influenced by an authority figure of superior status; and (c) the maintenance of social power and status of the authority figure in a hierarchical situation.

● A person commanded by a legitimate authority usually obeys – it is a ubiquitous and indispensable feature of social life.

● Obedience serves a number of productive functions, with the very survival of society depending on its existence.

Research method

- This study is generally considered a controlled observation. Although Milgram refers to the study as an experiment, there was in fact no independent variable.
- The study took place in a laboratory at Yale University, so conditions could be controlled – for example, who was teacher/learner; the learner's recorded and thus standardised responses; the experimenter's 'prods'.
- Data were gathered through observations made by both the experimenter, who was in the same room as the participant, and others who observed the process through one-way mirrors. Most sessions were recorded on magnetic tape; occasional photographs were taken through the one-way mirrors; and notes were made on unusual behaviours.
- Prior to the study, psychology students and professional colleagues estimated the percentage of participants who would administer the highest level of shock. Estimates ranged from 1 to 3 (mean 1.2).

- The adoption of the agentic state can account for horrific acts committed in the name of obedience – for example, the atrocities of the Second World War, the Balkans conflicts and the atrocities in Rwanda.
- The aim of this study was to investigate the process of obedience by testing how far an individual will go in obeying an authority figure, even when the command breaches the moral code that an individual should not hurt another person against his or her will.

Outline of the procedure/study

- Forty male participants, aged between 20 and 50 years, from the New Haven area in the USA, were obtained by a newspaper advertisement and direct-mail solicitation, which asked for volunteers to participate in a study of memory and learning at Yale University. There was a wide range of occupations in the sample. Participants were paid $4.50 for simply presenting themselves at the laboratory.
- Participants were always given the role of teacher (through a fixed lottery) and saw the learner (a confederate) strapped into a chair, with (non-active) electrodes attached to his arms. Participants were given a trial shock of 45 volts to simulate genuineness.
- The 'teacher' then sat in front of an electric shock generator in an adjacent room. He had to conduct a paired word test on the learner and give him an electric shock of increasing intensity for every wrong answer. The machine had 30 switches, ranging from 15 to 450 volts, in 15-volt increments.
- The 'learner' produced (via a tape recording) a set of predetermined responses, giving approximately three wrong answers to every correct one. At 300 volts he pounded on the wall and thereafter made no further replies.
- If the 'teacher' turned to the experimenter for advice on whether to proceed, the experimenter responded with a series of standardised prods – for example, 'Please continue'/'Please go on'.
- The study finished when the 'teacher' either refused to continue (was disobedient) or reached 450 volts (was obedient).
- The participant was then fully debriefed.

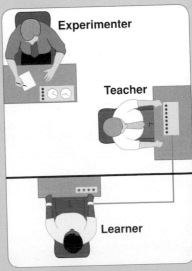

▲ **Figure 6.1** The room layout in the experiment

Key findings

- All participants 40/40 (100 per cent) continued to 300 volts.
- 26/40 (65 per cent) of participants continued to the full 450 volts.

▼ **Table 6.1** Distribution of break-off points for the 40 participants

No. of participants	Voltage/shock level
26	450
1	375
1	360
1	345
2	330
4	315
5	300

- Of the 40 participants, 26 were obedient, 14 disobedient.
- Many participants showed signs of extreme stress while administering the shocks – for example, sweating, trembling, stuttering, laughing nervously. Three had full-blown, uncontrollable seizures.
- On completion of the test, many obedient participants heaved sighs of relief, mopped their brows or nervously fumbled for cigarettes. Some shook their head, apparently in regret; some remained calm throughout.
- Milgram offered 13 possible explanations for the high levels of obedience shown by participants – for example, the fact that the study was carried out in the prestigious university of Yale influenced participants as to the worthiness of the study and the competence of the researcher; the participants were told the shocks were not harmful; the situation was completely new for the participants, so they had no past experience to guide their behaviour.

Conclusions

- Evil acts can be done by ordinary people.
- People will obey others whom they consider to be legitimate authority figures, even if what they are asked to do goes against their moral beliefs.
- People obey because certain situational features lead them to suspend their sense of autonomy and become agents of authority figures.
- Individual differences, such as personality, influence the extent to which people will be obedient.

Usefulness

- This study offers a useful explanation of why people obey in certain situations: if an individual is in a situation where s/he is asked to obey by a legitimate authority, s/he is likely to do so, even if it means acting against her/his own personal morality.
- The study is also useful as it shows that individuals are socialised to obey and so adds to the nature/nurture debate. In the light of this knowledge, it **should** be possible to ensure that malevolent social systems, such as the one that sanctioned the Holocaust in Nazi Germany, are never allowed to become dominant.

▲ **Figure 6.2** Milgram's shock generator

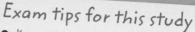

Issues to be considered

- Strengths/weaknesses of conducting research under controlled conditions.
- Strengths/weaknesses of snapshot studies.
- Strengths/weaknesses of observation and self-reports as ways to gather data.
- Strengths/weaknesses of quantitative and qualitative data.
- Strengths/weaknesses of the sample.
- Reliability.
- Validity and ecological validity.
- Ethics.

Exam tips for this study

- Know the research method and sample.
- Know the procedure in relation to 'teacher', 'learner' and experimenter.
- Know the key findings.
- Know at least three of Milgram's explanations for the results.
- Be able to draw conclusions from the findings.
- Be able to suggest at least one way in which the study could be improved, and possible implications of the suggestion(s) for methodology, ethics, reliability, validity, usefulness, practicality, and so on.

Exam-style questions linked to this study

Section A

1 (a) Identify **two** features of the sample. **[2]**

   (b) Outline **one** limitation of the sample. **[2]**

2 Describe how the sample was gathered. **[4]**

3 (a) Identify **two** ways in which the participants were deceived. **[4]**

   (b) Explain the benefits of deception as used in this study. **[2]**

4 (a) Outline **one** way in which this study may be considered high in ecological validity. **[2]**

   (b) Outline **one** way in which this study may be considered low in ecological validity. **[2]**

5 Describe why this study can be considered a controlled observation. **[4]**

6 (a) Describe **one** piece of quantitative data gathered in this study. **[2]**

   (b) Describe **one** piece of qualitative data gathered in this study. **[2]**

Section B

(a) Describe why this study was conducted. **[4]**

(b) With reference to this study, describe **one** strength and **one** weakness of quantitative data. **[6]**

(c) With reference to this study, describe **one** strength and **one** weakness of qualitative data. **[6]**

(d) Describe how obedience was measured in this study. **[6]**

(e) Outline **three** key findings of this study. **[6]**

(f) Describe ways in which this study could be improved. **[8]**

Section C

(a) Describe **one** assumption of the social approach. **[2]**

(b) Referring to this study, describe how the social approach can explain obedience. **[4]**

(c) Describe **one** similarity and **one** difference between any core studies that take the social approach. **[6]**

(d) Discuss strengths **and** weaknesses of the social approach, using examples from any of the core studies that take this approach. **[12]**

GROSS
PSYCHOLOGY
THE SCIENCE OF MIND AND BEHAVIOUR

pp. 413, 415

REICHER AND HASLAM (2006): BBC PRISON STUDY

Rethinking the psychology of tyranny. The BBC Prison Study

Background to the study

- The results of Zimbardo's (1973) Stanford Prison Experiment, which formed the basis for this study, led Zimbardo to suggest that social roles structure behaviour. In his study, the guards became extremely cruel and developed a 'pathology of power', as they saw themselves as having legitimate power over the prisoners. Prisoners, because of their insubordinate and inferior role, developed a 'pathological prisoner syndrome', demonstrated by increasingly negative behaviours and emotions.

- Reicher and Haslam challenged Zimbardo's explanation by suggesting that the concepts of social identity and social categorisation offer a more satisfactory explanation for group behaviour.

Relation to the social approach

- Social psychology is divided into two areas: social interaction (how individuals interact and how status in society influences behaviour); and social cognition (how thoughts and emotions about current social situations influence behaviour).
- This study focuses on the influence of social interaction and the effect of group identity and group inequalities on behaviour.
- The study shows oppression to be the product of active processes of social identification, which can also form the basis for both tyranny and resistance. Conflict, abuse and tyranny do not necessarily result from zombie-like compliance, but rather from individuals' active identification and engagement with the groups that promote them.

Theory/ies on which the study is based

- Reicher and Haslam argue that powerful and successful groups provide an effective psychological barrier against tyranny, and that it is when groups become ineffective that tyrannical forms of social organisation become attractive. (Tyranny = an unequal social system involving the arbitrary or oppressive use of power by one group or its agents over another.)

- Findings from Zimbardo's (1973) Stanford Prison Experiment suggested that in hierarchical situations, automatic deindividuation and conformity to social roles tends to lead groups to extreme antisocial or tyrannical behaviour, which helps to explain how we come to condone the tyranny of others or else act tyrannically ourselves.

- Reicher and Haslam proposed an alternative suggestion: a social identity approach – that is, people do not automatically act in terms of group membership or social roles, but only if they internalise the membership as part of their self-identity. Individuals who belong to a group behave in relation to the norms and values of the group, which may lead to either prosocial or antisocial behaviour. In a hierarchical social structure, dominant groups identify with their group and impose their power, whereas collective action by subordinate groups depends on the permeability of group boundaries and the security of intergroup relations.

Research method

● As Reicher and Haslam suggest, this study can be seen as an experimental case study.
● It was an experiment in that it was conducted in a controlled, specially designed environment, in a simulated prison constructed by the BBC at Elstree Studios, London. Extraneous variables were also controlled – for example, participants were matched for such characteristics as racism and authoritarianism, before being randomly allocated to roles of prisoner/guard, and given uniforms. Three independent variables (permeability of roles, legitimacy of roles and cognitive alternatives) were planned to be manipulated within the study.
● The dependent variables were:
  - social variables (social identification, awareness of cognitive alternatives, right-wing authoritarianism);
  - organisational variables (compliance with rules);
  - clinical variables (self-efficacy, depression).
● It was a case study because in-depth detailed data were collected on a very small sample (15 male participants) through direct observation by the researchers, analysis of video and audio recordings made throughout by the BBC, and daily psychometric and physiological measures to assess stress levels.

● They therefore created an environment that resembled various hierarchical institutions (e.g. prison, school, barracks), which would allow them to study the inequalities between groups in respect of power, status and resources.
● Their main predictions were that:
  - dominant group members would identify with their group – that is, guards would identify with their group and impose their power;
  - subordinate group members would only identify with their group and challenge intergroup inequalities if relations between the groups were considered impermeable and insecure.

Outline of the procedure/study

● The proposed procedure was submitted to various ethical committees (e.g. BPS), and was monitored throughout by independent psychologists and another ethics committee. Participants signed a comprehensive consent form.
● The study was planned to last for 10 days.
● Male participants were recruited through advertisements in the national press and leaflets. The initial pool of 332 was reduced to 27, through various screening processes. The final 15 were selected to show a diversity of age, social class and ethnic background. They were matched in threes on selected personality variables and randomly allocated two prisoners: one guard. One prisoner was not involved at the beginning of the study.
● Guards reported the evening before they entered the prison and were briefed about the study. The following morning they were taken to the prison in a blacked-out van and given further instructions. Prisoners arrived individually, had their heads shaved, were given basic uniforms, basic food and living conditions in lockable three-person cells. Guards had better uniforms, food and accommodation, plus control over keys and resources to use as rewards/punishments.
● There were three planned interventions:
  - permeability of roles;
  - legitimacy of roles (found to be unnecessary);
  - cognitive alternatives.
● The study was stopped on Day 8.
● Participants were fully debriefed on Day 9.

▲ **Figure 6.3** The participants in the study

Key findings

- Guards failed to internalise their role and failed to develop a group identity.
- Initially prisoners acted individually, to be promoted to the role of guard. Two prisoners (JE and KM) made particular efforts to be promoted.
- Once group impermeability was introduced, the prisoners began to develop a much stronger sense of shared identity and to develop more consensual norms. There was a move from compliance to conflict with the guards – for example, to see how the guards would respond, prisoner JE threw his lunch plate to the ground and demanded better food. They also began to envisage changes to the existing hierarchy and believe that they could achieve them.
- The natural development of insecure relations between the groups meant the planned intervention of legitimacy was not necessary, so was not implemented.
- The introduction of the new prisoner on Day 5 (a trade union official) was not needed to suggest cognitive alternatives as they had already surfaced; rather he was able to suggest additional alternatives to the status quo.
- On Day 6, dissent came to a head and some prisoners broke out of their cell and occupied the guards' quarters. The guards' regime therefore became unworkable.
- Terms for a new commune were drawn up, but within a day this was in crisis, because two ex-prisoners broke communal rules.
- A further, harsher prisoner–guard regime was proposed, but for ethical reasons could not be implemented, so the study was stopped.

Conclusions

- People do not automatically conform to group or social roles.
- Groups with power do not always act tyrannically.
- Failing, powerless groups can lead to tyranny.
- The breakdown of groups creates conditions under which tyranny can develop.

Usefulness

- As Zimbardo says, 'I want to thank these researchers for demonstrating a point that I have long argued in favour of as a means to reduce prisoner abuses, namely greater surveillance of guard–prisoner interactions. The BBC-TV research shows that such violence can be eliminated if all parties in a prison setting realize that their behaviour is open for scrutiny and evaluation' (Zimbardo, 2006).
- The main usefulness of this study, therefore, is that it implies that if adequate surveillance methods are implemented in prisons, the frequently reported instances of brutality and abuse within them could be reduced and possibly eliminated.
- The study also shows that if those in power do not identify with their group and enforce their authority in an organised and uniform way, subordinate groups, recognising this insecurity and lack of cohesion, may summon the necessary resources to challenge the situation.

Issues to be considered

- Strengths/weaknesses of laboratory experiments.
- Strengths/weaknesses of case studies.
- Strengths/weaknesses of observation and self-reports as ways to gather data.
- Strengths/weaknesses of quantitative and qualitative data.
- Strengths/weaknesses of the sample.
- Reliability.
- Validity and ecological validity.
- Ethics.

▲ **Figure 6.4**

Exam tips for this study

- Know the research method, the sample and how it was gathered.
- Know the procedure and how both guards and prisoners were introduced to the study.
- Know the three planned interventions.
- Know the key findings.
- Be able to draw conclusions from the findings.
- Be able to suggest at least one way in which the study could be improved, and possible implications of the suggestion(s) for methodology, ethics, reliability, validity, usefulness, practicality, and so on.

Exam-style questions linked to this study

Section A

1 Describe how the sample was selected. **[4]**
2 Describe the prison environment as constructed by the BBC. **[4]**
3 Describe how the guards were introduced to the study. **[4]**
4 (a) Describe **one** way in which this study had ecological validity. **[2]**
   (b) Describe **one** way in which this study lacked ecological validity. **[2]**
5 Outline **two** of the interventions planned for this study. **[4]**
6 (a) Describe **one** finding from this study. **[2]**
   (b) Suggest **one** conclusion that can be drawn from the findings of this study. **[2]**

Section B

(a) Outline the study on which this one was based. **[4]**
(b) Describe why the study can be considered a case study. **[4]**
(c) With reference to this study, describe **one** strength and **one** weakness of case studies. **[6]**
(d) Briefly discuss the validity of this study. **[6]**
(e) Suggest ways in which this study could be improved. **[8]**
(f) Consider the implications of the improvements you have suggested. **[8]**

Section C

(a) Outline the social approach. **[2]**
(b) Referring to this study, describe how the social approach might explain the development of tyranny. **[4]**
(c) Describe **one** similarity and **one** difference between any studies that take the social approach. **[6]**
(d) Discuss strengths **and** weaknesses of the social approach, using examples from any studies that take this approach. **[12]**

GROSS
PSYCHOLOGY
THE SCIENCE OF MIND AND BEHAVIOUR

p. 423

PILIAVIN *ET AL.* (1969): SUBWAY SAMARITAN

Good Samaritanism: An underground phenomenon?

▲ **Figure 6.5** Kitty Genovese

Background to the study

- Since the murder of Kitty Genovese in 1964 (a woman stabbed to death over a period of 30 minutes in front of 38 unresponsive witnesses), many social psychologists have studied the concept of Good Samaritanism.

- Research by Darley and Latané (1968) found that bystanders hearing an epileptic fit over earphones led to those who believed other witnesses were present being less likely to help the victim than bystanders who believed they were alone.

- Subsequent research by Latané and Rodin (1969), on the response to the victim of a fall, confirmed this finding, and suggested that assistance from bystanders was less likely if they were strangers than if they were acquaintances.

- Field experiments conducted by Bryan and Test (1967) showed that individuals are more likely to be Good Samaritans if they have just observed another individual performing a helpful act.

- Much of the work on victimisation has been conducted in laboratory settings, using non-visual emergency situations.

- This study was designed to investigate, under real-life conditions, the effect of several variables on helping behaviour.

Relation to the social approach

- One assumption of the social approach is that other people and the surrounding environment are major influences on an individual's behaviour, thought processes and emotions.

- The environment and situation we are in therefore have a major influence on whether or not individuals will help another person. Piliavin et al.'s study showed that when in a closed area, individuals tend not to diffuse responsibility by sharing it among those present; rather, they feel personally responsible, and so offer help to a victim in need of assistance. Findings from the study showed that the more people that were present when the incident occurred, the more people went to help the victim. They also found that the condition of a victim influenced helping behaviour: if a victim is lame, people are more likely to help than if a victim is drunk. Also, if a victim is the same race as a potential helper, they are more likely to help.

Theory/ies on which the study is based

- Although pluralistic ignorance and/or genuine ambiguity make it less likely that an individual will define a situation as an emergency, in many situations the reason an individual may not help is because they diffuse responsibility.

- Diffusion of responsibility is where the responsibility for the situation is spread (diffused) among the people present. This implies that the more people present, the more the bystander believes the responsibility is spread out, so s/he feels less personal responsibility and is therefore less likely to help.

- Another explanation for not helping a victim in need is that a bystander may believe that someone else will do what is necessary, so there is no need for them to offer assistance. This is known as 'bystander apathy'.

Research method

- The study was a field experiment.
- The field situation was the A and D trains of the 8th Avenue New York Subway, between 59th Street and 125th Street, a journey lasting about 7½ minutes.
- The experiment had four independent variables:
  - type of victim (drunk or carrying a cane);
  - race of victim (black or white);
  - effect of a model (after 70 or 150 seconds, from the critical or adjacent area), or no model at all;
  - size of the witnessing group (a naturally occurring independent variable).
- The dependent variables (recorded by two female observers seated in the adjacent area) were:
  - frequency of help;   - sex of helper
  - speed of help;   - movement out of critical area
  - race of helper;   - verbal comments by bystanders

Outline of the procedure/study

- Participants were about 4,500 men and women who used the subway on weekdays, between 11.00am and 3.00pm between 15 April and 26 June 1968. About 45 per cent were black, 55 per cent white.
- There were four teams of four researchers: two female observers, two males – one acting as the victim, one as the model.
- The victims (three white, one black) were all male, General Studies students, aged 26–35 years, and dressed alike. They either smelled of liquor and carried a liquor bottle wrapped tightly in a brown bag, or appeared sober and carried a black cane. In all aspects they acted identically in both conditions.
- The models (all white) were males aged 24–29 years. There were four model conditions:
  - critical area – early;   - adjacent area – early;
  - critical area – late;   - adjacent area – late.
- The observers recorded the dependent variables.
- The victim stood near a pole in the critical area. After about 70 seconds, he staggered forward and collapsed. Until receiving help, he remained supine on the floor, looking at the ceiling. If he received no help by the time the train stopped, the model helped him to his feet. At the stop, the team disembarked and waited separately until other passengers had left the station. They then changed platforms to repeat the process in the opposite direction.
- Between six and eight trials were run on a given day, all using the same 'victim condition'.

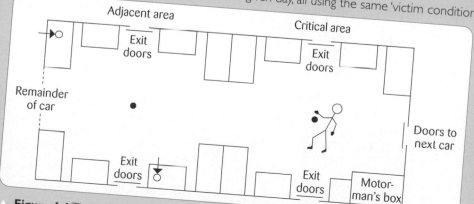

▲ **Figure 6.6** The layout of the train carriage

Key findings

- The cane victim received spontaneous help 95 per cent of the time (62/65 trials), compared to the drunk victim 50 per cent of the time (19/38 trials).
- Overall there was 100 per cent help for the cane victim, compared to 81 per cent help for the drunk victim.
- Help was offered more quickly to the cane victim (a median of 5 seconds compared to 109 seconds delay for the drunk victim).
- On 49/81 (60 per cent) trials, when help was given this was provided by two or more helpers.
- Of the first helpers, 90 per cent were males.
- There was a slight tendency for same-race helping, especially in the drunk condition.
- No diffusion of responsibility was found; in fact, response times were faster with larger groups than with smaller ones.
- More comments were made by passengers in the drunk than the cane condition, and most comments were made when no help was given within the first 70 seconds.

Conclusions

- An individual who appears ill is more likely to receive help than one who appears drunk.
- With mixed groups of men and women, men are more likely than women to help a male victim.
- With mixed-race groups, people are more likely to help those of the same race as themselves, particularly if they deem the victim's situation to be of his or her own making.
- There is no strong relationship between number of bystanders and speed of helping when an incident is visible.
- When escape is not possible and bystanders are face to face with a victim, help is likely to be forthcoming.
- Bystanders conduct a cost–reward analysis before deciding whether or not to help a victim.

Usefulness

- This study proposed a theoretical explanation to account for levels of helping, as helping behaviour is described in terms of the emotional and cognitive processes to which an individual responds when making a decision to offer assistance.
- It is useful to know that a bystander makes a cost–reward analysis before offering help to a victim, as it increases understanding of why people assist/fail to assist a person in need.
- The study also increases understanding of the situational effects on helping behaviour: if an individual witnesses an event from which they cannot escape, they are likely to offer assistance.

Issues to be considered

- Strengths/weaknesses of field experiments.
- Strengths/weaknesses of observation as a way to gather data.
- Strengths/weaknesses of snapshot and longitudinal studies.
- Strengths/weaknesses of quantitative and qualitative data.
- Strengths/weaknesses of the sample, victims, models and observers.
- Reliability.
- Validity and ecological validity.
- Ethics.

Exam tips for this study

- Know the research method and the field situation.
- Know the procedure in relation to the victim, model and observers.
- Know the key findings.
- Be able to draw conclusions from the findings.
- Be able to suggest at least one way in which the study could be improved, and possible implications of the suggestion(s) for methodology, ethics, reliability, validity, usefulness, practicality, and so on.

Exam-style questions linked to this study

Section A

1 **(a)** Describe the sample used in this study. **[2]**

  (b) Suggest **one** strength of this sample. **[2]**

2 Identify **four** independent variables measured in this study. **[4]**

3 Describe the victims in this study. **[4]**

5 Describe **two** findings from this study. **[4]**

6 **(a)** Describe the term diffusion of responsibility in relation to this study. **[2]**

  (b) Suggest why diffusion of responsibility was not found in this study. **[2]**

Section B

(a) Outline the incident that formed the basis for this study. **[2]**

(b) Outline how observation was used to gather data in this study. **[4]**

(c) With reference to this study, describe **one** strength and **one** weakness of observation as a way to gather data. **[6]**

(d) Outline the procedure followed in this study. **[8]**

(e) Describe key findings of this study. **[8]**

(f) Suggest **two** ways this study could be improved, and consider the implications of your suggestions. **[8]**

Section C

(a) Describe **one** implication of the social approach. **[2]**

(b) Referring to this study, describe how the social approach might explain helping behaviour. **[4]**

(c) Describe **one** similarity and **one** difference between this study and any other core study that takes the social approach. **[6]**

(d) Discuss strengths **and** weaknesses of the social approach, using examples from this study to support your answer. **[12]**

pp. 468–71

ROSENHAN (1973): ON BEING SANE IN INSANE PLACES

Background to the study

- Benedict (1934) suggested that normality and abnormality are not universal – what is viewed as normal in one culture may be considered abnormal in another.

- The general belief is that patients present symptoms, the symptoms can be categorised, and therefore the sane are distinguishable from the insane. However, this belief has been questioned.

- The view has grown that psychological categorisation of mental illness is useless at best, and harmful and misleading at worst. Psychiatric diagnoses are seen to be in the minds of the observers and are not valid summaries of characteristics displayed by the observed.

- The question is therefore: can the sane be distinguished from the insane? Do the characteristics that lead to diagnosis lie in the patients themselves or in the

Relation to the individual differences approach

- Individuals are unique, so differ in their behaviour and personal qualities. Not everyone can therefore be considered 'the average person'.

- The individual differences approach could explain abnormality, because although the approach assumes that everyone is different, it is generally held that people demonstrating or reporting behaviour deemed atypical/ outside the norm accepted by any given society are considered abnormal. This was shown in the Rosenhan study, when the pseudopatients reported hearing voices that said, 'empty', 'hollow' and 'thud'. This is not behaviour reported by the average person and was therefore considered abnormal. Using criterion set down in the DSM II, which categorises certain behaviours to be outside the continuum of normality, these pseudopatients were diagnosed as either schizophrenic or manic depressive – types of insanity/ abnormality. Their individual differences meant they were labelled as abnormal.

Theory/ies on which the study is based

- Different criteria for defining normality/abnormality propose how and where a line can be drawn between the two.

- Abnormality can be seen as any of: a deviation from the average, a deviation from the norm, a deviation from ideal mental health, personal distress, others' distress, maladaptiveness, unexpected behaviour, highly predictable/unpredictable behaviour, mental illness.

- To be diagnosed as 'abnormal' requires a classification system against which an individual's patterns of behaviour or mental symptoms can be measured.

- For classification systems to be reliable, different diagnosticians using the same system should arrive at the same diagnosis for the same individual. The reliability of early systems, such as the DSM II, was very poor.

Research method

- Rosenhan reports on three studies: two are usually considered as participant observations, the third a self-report.
- In Study 1(a), Rosenhan controlled the pseudopatients' procedure for gaining admission to hospital. Once admitted, pseudopatients gathered data by observing behaviours of staff and genuine patients, and recorded observations in notebooks. Reports produced both quantitative and qualitative data.
- In Study 1(b), Rosenhan controlled the questions asked of staff by pseudopatients, and made sure that any one member of staff was never approached more than once a day. Pseudopatients observed and recorded responses. This produced both quantitative and qualitative data.
- In Study 2, Rosenhan used the self-report method, asking staff to rate prospective patients on the likelihood that they were a pseudopatient. A 10-point scale was used, with 1 and 2 reflecting high confidence that the person was a pseudopatient. Results were analysed, providing quantitative data.

environments and contexts in which observers find them? The question of disposition versus situation can be investigated by getting normal people admitted to psychiatric hospitals. If these 'pseudopatients' are diagnosed as sane, then a sane individual can be identified in the insane context in which s/he is found, but if s/he is diagnosed as insane, it can be suggested that it is the context rather than the pseudopatient's characteristics that determine the diagnosis.

- Rosenhan aimed to illustrate:
  - the poor reliability of the diagnostic system at the time (DSM II, introduced in 1968);
  - the negative consequences of being diagnosed as insane and the effects of institutionalisation.

Outline of the procedure/study

Study 1(a)

- Eight pseudopatients (five men, three women), from a minority of occupations, using fake names and occupations, sought admission to 12 hospitals (of varying ages, resources and staff ratios) across five states in the USA.
- Pseudopatients arranged an appointment at the hospital and on arrival reported that they had been hearing voices that were unclear, unfamiliar, of the same sex as themselves, and said, 'empty', 'hollow' and 'thud'.
- Once admitted, pseudopatients behaved normally, interacted with staff and patients and participated in ward activities. During their internment they observed the behaviour of staff and genuine patients and recorded their observations in a notebook.
- Pseudopatients had the responsibility of persuading hospital staff that they were sane and could therefore be discharged.

Study 1(b)

- In four of the hospitals, pseudopatients approached members of staff and asked, 'Pardon me Mr/Dr/Mrs X, could you tell me when I will be eligible for grounds privileges / ...when will I be presented at the staff meeting / ...when am I likely to be discharged?'
- Pseudopatients observed the responses and recorded them in their notebooks.

Study 2

- Staff at a psychiatric hospital who were aware of the findings of the first study were warned that pseudopatients would present themselves over the next three months. None actually did so.
- Staff were asked to rate each patient who arrived at admissions/the ward, according to the likelihood that s/he was a pseudopatient.

Key findings

Study 1(a)

- All pseudopatients were admitted and all bar one were diagnosed as schizophrenic. Each was eventually discharged with schizophrenia 'in remission'.
- Length of hospitalisation ranged from 7 to 52 days (average 19 days).
- Many real patients detected the pseudopatients' sanity – 35/118 genuine patients voiced their suspicions in the first three hospitalisations.
- Normal behaviour was misinterpreted – for example, writing extensive notes was once reported as 'patient engages in writing behaviours'; pacing the hospital corridors through boredom was a sign of anxiety; queuing early for lunch was observed by one psychiatrist as a characteristic of the oral-acquisitive nature of their syndrome.
- Personal hygiene and waste evacuation were often monitored. Water closets had no doors.
- Average daily contact with medical staff ranged from 3.9 to 25.1 minutes (mean 6.8 minutes).
- All pseudopatients experienced powerlessness and depersonalisation.

Study 1(b)

- The most common response was either a brief response offered while they were 'on the move', with head averted, or no response at all.
- Few staff made eye contact with pseudopatients.

Study 2

- A total of 193 patients reported for psychiatric treatment.
- Of these, 41 were judged by at least one member of staff, 23 by at least one psychiatrist, and 19 by at least two members of staff, to be pseudopatients.

Conclusions

- The sane cannot be distinguished from the insane in psychiatric hospitals.
- Patients in psychiatric hospitals experience powerlessness and depersonalisation.
- Once a patient has been labelled 'insane', all subsequent behaviour is seen in the light of the label given.
- Institutionalisation in psychiatric hospitals has negative effects on interred patients.
- Mental health workers are insensitive to the feelings and emotions of psychiatric patients.
- The DSM II had poor reliability.

Usefulness

- This study highlighted the deficiencies of the classification system for mental disorder at the time (DSM II), and the negative effects of being labelled and institutionalised for psychiatric disorders. It led to pressure being exerted on organisations such as the American Psychiatric Association to review and revise the accuracy of the classification systems; the DSM IV-TR (text revision) was introduced in 2000.
- The study helped to increase the sensitivity of health workers, making them more aware of the feelings and emotions of their patients.
- Awareness of the negative effects of institutionalisation has encouraged the development of other approaches to the treatment of psychiatric disorders, including the provision of community mental health facilities.

Issues to be considered

- Strengths/weaknesses of field experiments.
- Strengths/weaknesses of observation and self-reports as ways to gather data.
- Strengths/weaknesses of longitudinal studies.
- Strengths/weaknesses of quantitative and qualitative data.
- Strengths/weaknesses of the sample.
- Reliability.
- Validity and ecological validity.
- Ethics.

▲ **Figure 7.1**

Exam-style questions linked to this study

Section A

1 (a) Identify **two** features of the pseudopatients in this study. **[2]**
  (b) Outline **one** weakness of the pseudopatients used in this study. **[2]**
2 Describe how pseudopatients gained admittance to hospitals in Study 1. **[4]**
3 Outline **two** examples of how normal behaviour was misinterpreted in Study 1. **[4]**
4 Draw **two** conclusions from the findings of Study 1.**[4]**
5 Outline the procedure followed in Study 2. **[4]**
6 Describe **two** ethical issues that could be raised against these studies. **[4]**

Section B

(a) Describe the aim of these studies. **[2]**
(b) Describe how data were gathered in these studies. **[4]**
(c) With reference to these studies, describe **one** strength and **one** weakness of observational studies. **[6]**
(d) Outline the findings of these studies. **[8]**
(e) Suggest ways in which these studies could be improved. **[8]**
(f) Consider implications of the improvements you have suggested. **[8]**

Section C

(a) Describe **one** implication of the individual differences approach. **[2]**
(b) Referring to this study, describe how the individual differences approach could explain insanity. **[4]**
(c) Describe **one** similarity and **one** difference between these studies and any other core studies that take the individual differences approach. **[6]**
(d) Discuss strengths **and** weaknesses of the individual differences approach, using examples from Rosenhan's studies to support your answer. **[12]**

GROSS

THE SCIENCE OF MINDS AND BEHAVIOUR

pp. 682–6, 688–91

THIGPEN AND CLECKLEY (1954): THE THREE FACES OF EVE

A case of multiple personality

▲ **Figure 7.2** An image from the film adaptation of Thigpen and Cleckley's study

Background to the study

● In the 1950s, MPD was rarely identified or documented, even though it was a reasonably well-known psychiatric disorder. There were few detailed case histories (e.g. Morton Price's study of Miss Beauchamp, 1906) and these were viewed with considerable suspicion.

● Christine Sizemore (Eve White) was initially referred to Thigpen because of 'severe and blinding headaches', which appeared to have no physical cause. 'Blackouts' often followed the headaches, but the receipt of an unsigned letter, clearly started by Eve White because of the handwriting, but which had obviously different writing in the final paragraph, led Thigpen and Cleckley (both psychiatrists working to help people with psychological problems) to suspect the patient was suffering from MPD.

● Their study is therefore an account of the psychotherapeutic treatment of Eve White.

Relation to the individual differences approach

● The individual differences approach is concerned with the ways in which people can differ from one another.

● It includes personality, intelligence and psychological abnormality. Major mental disorders include schizophrenia, depression, anxiety disorders and eating disorders.

● Thigpen and Cleckley's study is concerned with the psychological disorder multiple personality disorder (MPD), known in the USA as dissociative identity disorder (DID).

● Individual differences is a 'person approach', which makes great use of field studies and non-experimental methods (e.g. observation, correlation).

Theory/ies on which the study is based

- MPD is a mental disorder characterised by having at least one other personality (alter), which, at times, controls an individual's behaviour.
- MPD should not be confused with schizophrenia, as sufferers of MPD do not experience the emotional and cognitive disturbances typical of schizophrenia.
- In MPD, individually each personality has distinct memories, its own social relationships, individual behaviour patterns and its own cognitive functionings. These differences are illustrated in this study.
- Dissociation produces a lack of connection in a person's thoughts, memories, feelings, actions or sense of identity, all of which are shown in this study. Although there are distinct 'entities' within a person, they are all manifestations of the same person.
- MPD is believed to be a response to extremely traumatic situations from which the individual has no physical means of escape. Traumatic situations might involve childhood abuse or emotional pain caused by witnessing a stressful event. If the person dissociates themselves from the situation, they can function as if it had not occurred.

Research method

- This was a longitudinal case study.
- A case study is a research method involving the detailed study of either a single individual or a very small group of individuals, an institution or an event.
- Here, the three personalities, Eve White, Eve Black and Jane, were studied in depth, using a variety of investigative measures – observation, hypnosis, self-reports, reports from family members and psychological testing – to produce extremely detailed information.
- The study is considered longitudinal because it covers a period of 14 months, during which Eve White/Eve Black/Jane were interviewed for approximately 100 hours.

Outline of the procedure/study

- Eve White was initially interviewed irregularly. During this time it became obvious that she had a number of emotional problems.
- After one visit, the researchers received a letter which, although unsigned, because of the penmanship, had clearly been started by Eve White. Eve White did not remember ending the letter, and its final paragraph looked as though it had been written by a child.
- Eve White's husband also reported that Eve had been behaving in a strange manner – for example, going into town and buying an array of expensive clothes, which was completely out of character.
- During the next interview, Eve White showed signs of stress and agitation, which prompted the appearance of Eve Black. The new Eve explained that the blackouts Eve White suffered were when she was 'out', but that Eve White had no awareness of her.
- Over the next 14 months, both Eves were interviewed for approximately 100 hours in total.
- Initially, Eve White had to be hypnotised to let Eve Black 'out', but over time she came out when called.
- Both personalities were very different: Eve White was demure, retiring, neat, colourless, honest and serious; Eve Black was mischievous, childish, a party girl, egocentric and provocative.
- After 8 months Eve White seemed to have made progress, but then the headaches and blackouts returned.
- At one of the therapy sessions, while talking about her childhood, she became sleepy, and Jane emerged. She was aware of both Eves, but was distinctly different, being mature, sincere, capable and interesting. She seemed to be the most balanced personality of the three.

Key findings

- Not long into therapy, Eve explained that she heard voices that were becoming more and more frequent, and expressed a fear that she was going mad. This prompted the appearance of the second personality – Eve Black. After this, the headaches and blackouts improved.

- After 8 months of therapy, the situation changed for the worse. Eve White's headaches and blackouts returned. During one session of hypnosis, the third person – Jane – appeared.

- Jane appeared to be the most balanced of the three personalities, and the one Thigpen and Cleckley felt should be encouraged to take over. However, they realised that it was not their responsibility to make this decision, and this study ends with the three faces of Eve still in existence.

- Results of the psychological tests:
  - IQ test: EW 110, EB 104.
  - Memory scales: EW had a superior memory function to EB.
  - Rorschach test (inkblot test): EW was emotionally repressed, EB had a tendency to regress.

- Results of the EEG test:
  - Tenseness was most pronounced in EB, next EW and then Jane.
  - EW and Jane: 11 cycles per second (normal), EB: 12.5 cycles per second (slightly fast, sometimes associated with psychopathic personality).

▲ **Figure 7.3** An inkblot

Conclusions

- Thigpen and Cleckley concluded that Eve White/Christine Sizemore was suffering from MPD. They did admit the possibility that Eve was just an extremely skilful actress and was actually faking the different personalities. However, they thought this highly unlikely, given the extreme length of time spent interviewing, observing and testing the three personalities.

- Thigpen and Cleckley were convinced that the study demonstrated a clear case of MPD, rather than any other hysterical conversion or dissociation.

Usefulness

- Findings showed support for the origins of MPD being the result of traumatic childhood experiences and therefore increased understanding of both this disorder and the effects of negative physical and emotional experiences.

- However, both the BPS and the Royal College of Physicians warn that therapists can easily encourage false memories of childhood abuse and that the memories of patients with dissociation may be unreliable.

- Diagnosis has been used successfully as a legal defence, on occasions (e.g. Arthur Wayne Bicknell, 1976). However, the use of MPD as a legal defence remains a controversial issue.

Issues to be considered

- Strengths/weaknesses of case studies.
- Strengths/weaknesses of longitudinal studies.
- Strengths/weaknesses of self-reports.
- Strengths/weaknesses of observations.
- Strengths/weaknesses of the sample.
- Strengths/weaknesses of quantitative and qualitative data.
- Reliability.
- Validity and ecological validity.
- Ethics.

Exam tips for this study

- Know the research method and how data were gathered.
- Know the key characteristics of each personality.
- Be able to draw conclusions from the findings.
- Be able to suggest at least one way in which the study could be improved, and possible implications of the suggestion(s) for methodology, ethics, reliability, validity, usefulness, practicality, and so on.

Exam-style questions linked to this study

Section A

1 Outline **two** features of multiple personality disorder. **[4]**
2 **(a)** Describe the research method used in this study. **[2]**
  (b) Suggest **one** strength of the research method used in this study. **[2]**
3 Outline **two** of the personalities identified in this study. **[4]**
4 **(a)** Identify **two** psychological tests used in this study. **[2]**
  (b) Outline the findings of **one** of the psychological tests used in this study. **[2]**
5 Outline the results of the electroencephalogram (EEG) conducted in this study. **[4]**
6 Describe **two** pieces of evidence that indicate Eve was suffering from MPD. **[4]**

Section B

(a) What was the aim of this study? **[2]**
(b) Describe why the sample was chosen and suggest one disadvantage of this sample. **[6]**
(c) Describe **two** advantages of the case study method as used by Thigpen and Cleckley. **[6]**
(d) Describe **two** disadvantages of the case study method as used by Thigpen and Cleckley. **[6]**
(e) Outline the findings of this study. **[8]**
(f) Suggest, with reasons, how this study could be improved. **[8]**

Section C

(a) Outline **one** assumption of the individual differences approach. **[2]**
(b) With reference to this study, describe how the individual differences approach could explain multiple personality disorder. **[4]**
(c) Describe **one** similarity and **one** difference between any studies that take the individual differences approach. **[6]**
(d) Discuss strengths **and** weaknesses of the individual differences approach, using examples from any studies that take this approach. **[12]**

GROSS
PSYCHOLOGY
THE SCIENCE OF MIND AND BEHAVIOUR

pp. 682–90

GRIFFITHS (1994): COGNITIVE BIAS IN GAMBLING

The role of cognitive bias and skill in fruit machine gambling

Background to the study

● Corney and Cummings (1985) noted that gamblers tend to exhibit rather consistent biases when processing information cognitively.

● Research has shown that the most salient cognitive distortions are: the illusion of control, hindsight bias, flexible attributions, representative bias, availability bias, illusory correlations and fixation on absolute frequency, all of which can be related to gambling. These heuristics were considered by Wagenaar (1988) as the best way of understanding cognitive processes in relation to gambling.

Relation to the individual differences approach

● Every individual is genetically unique and this uniqueness is displayed through their behaviour, so everyone behaves differently.

● This approach can explain gambling, because it focuses on differences rather than commonalities between people. Griffiths, in his study into fruit machine gambling, looked at the behaviours of regular and non-regular gamblers. He found that regular gamblers were more likely than non-regular gamblers to personalise the machine, by saying such things as, 'The machine likes me', and to make more irrational vocalisations than non-regular gamblers, such as 'I lost because I wasn't concentrating'. Such behaviours show that regular gamblers behave differently to non-regular gamblers, implying that individual differences are strong factors affecting gambling behaviour.

Theory/ies on which the study is based

● Addiction is an attachment to an appetitive activity, so strong that a person finds it difficult to moderate the activity, despite the fact that it is causing harm (Orford, 2001).

● Addiction is usually explained by applying one of three models of behaviour: the biological/cognitive/learning models.

● Griffiths leans towards the use of the cognitive model to explain gambling behaviours. Two approaches have been used to explain the cognitive processes involved in gambling: (i) normative decision-making (ii) heuristics and biases.

● Normative decision-making assumes that decisions made by gamblers will be rational. However, research does not support this and suggests that many decisions and choices made by gamblers are actually irrational.

● Wagenaar (1988) suggested that gambling behaviours are best explained by the selection of the wrong heuristics and inappropriate cognitive biases. He suggested that there were 16 distortions/biases that operate in gambling situations.

Research method

- This was a quasi/natural field experiment, which used an independent measures design. Self-reports and content analysis were used to analyse data.
- The field situation was an amusement arcade in Plymouth, Devon.
- It was a quasi/natural experiment because the independent variable – being a gambler (an individual who gambled at least once a week) or a non-gambler (someone who had used a fruit machine at least once, but who gambled once a month or less) could not be manipulated by the researcher.
- The dependent variables were the behavioural measures of gambling.
- Content analysis, involving a coding system for 31 categories of statements (including rational and irrational verbalisations), was used to analyse data through the 'thinking aloud method'.
- Self-reports in the post-experimental semi-structured interviews gathered information on the subjective skill perceptions of RGs and NRGs.

- Griffiths (1990) found that regular fruit machine gamblers used various heuristics during gambling, particularly to explain losses or bad gambling. They also believed their actions to be at least partly based on skill, and that they gained a sense of control through familiarity with a particular machine.

- In this study, Griffiths examined:
  - whether the skill involved in fruit machine gambling is 'actual' or perceived, by comparing the success of regular (RG) and non-regular (NRG) gamblers;
  - the cognitive activities of RGs and NRGs while gambling on fruit machines, using the 'thinking aloud method';
  - subjective measures of skill and skill perception in RGs and NRGs, using a post-experimental semi-structured interview.

Outline of the procedure/study

- Sixty individuals (44 males, 16 females), mean age 23.4 years, were recruited via a small poster advertisement circulated around Plymouth University and college campuses, with a number of RGs being recruited by an RG known to Griffiths. There were 30 RGs (29 males, 1 female), mean age 21.6 years, and 30 NRGs (15 males, 15 females), mean age 25.3 years.
- Each participant was given £3 (the equivalent of 30 free gambles) and was asked to stay on the machine for a minimum of 60 gambles (to break even and win back the £3). Any participant who achieved 60 gambles with the initial stake had the choice of keeping the winnings or continuing gambling.
- All participants were asked to gamble on a particular machine (i.e. FRUITSKILL), chosen by Griffiths as an experimental control.
- All RGs and NRGs were randomly allocated to either the 'thinking aloud' or the 'non-thinking aloud' condition.
- Those in the 'thinking aloud' condition had to continuously report everything that went through their minds as they gambled. Verbalisations were recorded via lapel microphones and transcribed by Griffiths within 24 hours.
- All participants then took part in a post-experimental interview, which contained a number of questions relating to skill – for example, 'Is there any skill involved in playing a fruit machine?'
- Participants in the 'thinking aloud' condition were asked if they would like to hear a playback of their recording.

▲ **Figure 7.4**

Key findings

- RGs had a significantly higher playing rate than NRGs – eight gambles: six gambles per minute.
- RGs who thought aloud had a significantly lower win rate in number of gambles than NRGs – that is, the number of gambles between each win was lower for NRGs.
- RGs stayed on the fruit machine longer than NRGs using the initial stake, in terms of the number of gambles.
- There was no significant difference between the playing times of RGs and NRGs.
- RGs produced significantly more irrational verbalisations than NRGs.
- NRGs produced significantly more verbalisations in questions of confusion and non-understanding than RGs.
- The majority of verbalisations for both RGs and NRGs were rational.
- Most RGs believed gambling on fruit machines was 'equal chance and skill', whereas most NRGs said 'mostly chance'.
- RGs claimed they were at least of average skill, whereas most NRGs viewed themselves as 'below average skill' or 'totally unskilled'.
- Fourteen RGs managed to break even on the initial stake, compared to seven NRGs.
- Ten RGs carried on gambling until they had lost everything, compared to two NRGs.

Conclusions

- There is little or no skill involved in fruit machine gambling.
- People who verbalise their thoughts while gambling take longer to gamble on fruit machines than people who do not think aloud while gambling.
- RGs are more skill-orientated than NRGs.
- The main difference between RGs and NRGs in relation to skill is probably cognitive.
- There is a cognitive difference in how RGs and NRGs react towards fruit machines.
- Cognitive distortions may underlie gambling behaviours.

Usefulness

- Knowledge of an irrational gambling bias may help in rehabilitating gamblers through cognitive behaviour modification (Griffiths, 1990; Strumphauzer, 1980). This would involve the attempt to modify the thought patterns of an individual, in an attempt to moderate or stop their gambling. This might be done by using a similar process to the one used here, by playing back tape recordings of a pathological gambler thinking aloud to highlight their irrational cognitions.
- Availability bias, illusory correlations and illusions of control can help explain the persistence of gambling (Griffiths, 1997b).
- Although, to date, there are no reports of cognitive restructuring being used in this way, Walker (1992b) identified six strategies employed by slot machine gamblers. If a therapist can establish a detailed structure of a persistent gambler, including their use of these strategies and their thoughts while gambling, s/he can begin to moderate or eliminate the motivation to gamble.

Issues to be considered

- Strengths/weaknesses of field experiments.
- Strengths/weaknesses of an independent measures design.
- Strengths/weaknesses of snapshot studies.
- Strengths/weaknesses of self-reports and content analysis as ways to gather and analyse data.
- Strengths/weaknesses of quantitative and qualitative data.
- Strengths/weaknesses of the sample.
- Reliability.
- Validity and ecological validity.
- Ethics.

▲ **Figure 7.5**

Exam-style questions linked to this study

Section A

1 (a) Describe how the sample was gathered. **[2]**
   (b) Outline **one** limitation of the way the sample was gathered. **[2]**
2 Describe the task given to participants. **[4]**
3 (a) Describe the term 'content analysis' in relation to this study. **[2]**
   (b) Outline **one** weakness of content analysis as used in this study. **[2]**
4 (a) Describe the purpose of the post-experimental semi-structured interviews. **[2]**
   (b) Outline **one** finding from these interviews. **[2]**
5 (a) Describe **one** finding that showed a similarity in the performance of RGs and NRGs. **[2]**
   (b) Describe **one** finding that showed a difference in performance between RGs and NRGs. **[2]**
6 Briefly describe why the findings of this study may not be reliable. **[4]**

Section B

(a) Describe **one** aim of this study. **[2]**
(b) Explain why this study is considered a quasi/natural field experiment. **[6]**
(c) With reference to this study, describe **one** strength and **one** weakness of field experiments. **[6]**
(d) Describe the procedure used in this study. **[8]**
(e) Briefly discuss ethical issues in relation to this study. **[8]**
(f) Suggest ways in which this study could be improved. **[8]**

Section C

(a) Outline the individual differences approach. **[2]**
(b) Referring to this study, describe how the individual differences approach might explain gambling addiction. **[4]**
(c) Describe **one** similarity and **one** difference between this study and any other studies that take the individual differences approach. **[6]**
(d) Discuss strengths **and** weaknesses of the individual differences approach, using examples from any of the core studies that take this approach. **[12]**

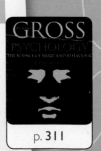

GROSS
PSYCHOLOGY
THE SCIENCE OF MIND AND BEHAVIOUR

p. 311

THE BEHAVIOURIST PERSPECTIVE

Background to the perspective

The behaviourist perspective assumes that all individuals are born as blank slates, and that all behaviour is learned through experiences after birth. It is also often referred to as either the learning perspective or environmental determinism, because the assumption is that behaviour is determined by past experiences. Psychologists therefore suggest that learning is 'a relatively permanent change in behaviour due to past experience'.

The behaviourist school was established in 1913 by J.B. Watson, in an attempt to establish psychology as a science. This therefore meant that psychological research should focus on things that could be assessed objectively rather than inferred. Watson proposed that psychologists should confine themselves to studying behaviour, since only this is actually measurable and observable by more than one person.

Behaviourism was the dominant force in psychology for over 40 years, until the late 1950s, when many British and American psychologists began looking to the work of computer scientists in an attempt to understand more complex behaviours, which, they felt, had been oversimplified by learning theories.

Behaviourism holds that stimulus–response units of behaviour are learned as a result of experiences and interactions with the environment, and that these then determine what an individual is and how they behave. All behaviour can therefore be explained in terms of conditioning to produce the stimulus–response links, which in turn build into more complex behaviours.

There are three sub-strands of behaviourism: *classical conditioning*, *operant conditioning* and *social learning theory* (though it is now acknowledged that this can involve elements of cognition).

▲ **Figure 8.1** J.B. Watson

Theories linked to the perspective

The key form of learning is *conditioning*, either *classical* (Pavlovian) or *operant* (instrumental – the centre of Skinner's form of behaviourism).

Classical conditioning theory (Pavlov)

In classical conditioning, a stimulus is seen as a predictable and automatic cue to trigger a response. It is concerned with learning by association, and refers to the conditioning of reflexes. The principles of classical conditioning were first outlined by Pavlov.

Operant conditioning

Operant conditioning is concerned with learning through the consequences of behavioural responses. The principles of operant conditioning were first investigated by Thorndike (1898), who found that any response that resulted in desirable consequences was more likely to be repeated than any response that resulted in undesirable consequences. This principle became known as the Law of Effect.

Skinner (1938, 1948a, 1948b) developed his own version of the Law of Effect and proposed that 'behaviour is shaped and maintained by its consequences'. The consequences of operants can be positive reinforcement, negative reinforcement or punishment.

Social learning theory (SLT)

Classical and operant conditioning ignore any cognitive factors between the stimulus and response that can influence learning. Skinner's claim that reinforcements and punishments *automatically* strengthen and weaken behaviour was challenged by Bandura (1977a), who proposed that 'reinforcements served principally as an informative and motivational operation, rather than as a mechanical response strengthener'. His cognitive reinterpretation of reinforcement formed part of his social learning theory (SLT), which focuses on observational learning. Whilst not denying the role of both classical and operant conditioning, SLT focuses on observational learning (or modelling), in which cognitive factors are crucial. This is reflected in Bandura's renaming (1986,1989) of SLT as *social cognitive theory*.

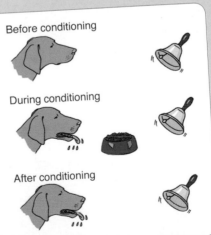

Before conditioning

During conditioning

After conditioning

▲ **Figure 8.2** Pavlov's classical conditioning

ISSUES TO BE CONSIDERED

Strengths of the behaviourist perspective

✔ Its objective and standardised methodology allows possible confounding variables to be controlled, making studies easy to replicate, so reliability can be checked.

✔ It is very scientific and usually uses controlled experimental methods, so cause and effect can be inferred.

✔ Because it highlights the role of nurture in learning, and shows the important influence that environmental factors have on behaviour, it provides a strong counter-argument to the nature side of the nature/ nurture debate.

✔ It assumes that if behaviour can be learned, it can be unlearned, which implies that behaviour can be controlled and changed if desired.

✔ It is reductionist, as it allows the researcher to focus on the influence of one factor – nurture – on behaviour.

✔ The focus on studying observable behaviour in laboratory experiments gave psychology as a discipline the scientific credibility it previously lacked.

▲ **Figure 8.3** The behaviourist perspective relies heavily on animal studies, raising problems with generalisability and ethical issues

Weaknesses of the behaviourist perspective

✘ It is reductionist, as it ignores the influences of nature and cognition on behaviour.

✘ The emphasis on objectivity and standardisation means that most behaviourist studies are laboratory experiments. This means they lack ecological validity, so findings may not reflect behaviours that people demonstrate in real-life situations.

✘ The perspective in general raises moral and ethical issues: if behaviour can be changed/unlearned through conditioning and/or observation, who should have the right to decide which behaviours should be changed, and why?

✘ Studies that can be viewed from this perspective often raise ethical issues, particularly in relation to long- and short-term psychological harm.

✘ This perspective relies heavily on findings from animal studies, which open up the ethical debate concerning the use of animals in scientific/psychological research.

✘ The reliance on animal studies poses problems when trying to generalise findings to humans.

Exam-style questions linked to the behaviourist perspective

Section C

(a)

(i) Outline the behaviourist perspective. **[2]**
(ii) Describe **one** assumption of the behaviourist perspective. **[2]**
(iii) Describe **one** implication of the behaviourist perspective. **[2]**

▲ **Figure 8.4** The behaviourist perspective sees children as blank slates, with all behaviour being learned through experience

▲ **Figure 8.5** How might the behaviourist perspective explain aggression?

(b)

(i) Describe how the behaviourist perspective could explain aggression. **[4]**
(ii) Describe how the behaviourist perspective might explain obedience. **[4]**
(iii) Describe how the behaviourist perspective could explain helping behaviour. **[4]**
(iv) Describe how the behaviourist perspective might explain gambling behaviour. **[4]**

(c)

(i) Describe **one** similarity and **one** difference between any studies that can be viewed from the behaviourist perspective. **[6]**
(ii) Describe **one** similarity and **one** difference between any core studies that could be viewed from the behaviourist perspective. **[6]**

(d)

(i) Discuss strengths **and** weaknesses of the behaviourist perspective, using examples from any studies that can be viewed from this perspective. **[12]**
(ii) Discuss strengths **and** weaknesses of the behaviourist perspective, using examples from any of the core studies that might be viewed from this perspective. **[12]**

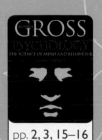

GROSS
PSYCHOLOGY
THE SCIENCE OF MIND AND BEHAVIOUR

pp. 2, 3, 15–16

THE PSYCHODYNAMIC PERSPECTIVE

Background to the perspective

Sigmund Freud, born in Austria in 1856, is the main person involved in this perspective, with some of his followers breaking away to develop their own theories – for example, Jung, Adler, Klein, Anna Freud (Freud's daughter) and Erikson. Freud distinguished between two mental states – the conscious and the unconscious. The conscious mind is the state when individuals are aware of their motivations for behaviour that they can then explain verbally, whereas the unconscious mind is the state when behavioural motivations are often complex and related to sex in some way. These are largely hidden from an individual's conscious mind, but are actually the driving force behind visible behaviour.

The term psychodynamic denotes the active forces within an individual's personality that motivate behaviour, and the inner causes of behaviour (in particular the unconscious conflict between the different components of personality).

Freud became convinced that unconscious mental causes of behaviour were responsible for many psychological disorders. He developed psychoanalysis – a set of techniques for treating the unconscious causes of mental disorders – which has had a great impact on psychology and psychiatry.

▲ **Figure 9.1** Sigmund Freud

Theories linked to the perspective

Freud's (tripartite) personality theory

Freud believed that personality comprises three parts: the *id*, *ego* and *superego*. The id 'contains everything that is inherited, that is present at birth, that is laid down in constitution – above all, therefore, the instincts' (Freud, 1923). The ego is 'that part of the *id* which has been modified by the direct influence of the external world' (Freud, 1923). The superego 'observes the *ego*, gives it orders, judges it and threatens it with punishment, exactly like the parents whose place it has taken' (Freud, 1933).

Ego-defence mechanisms

Freud believed that conflict within the three components of personality is unavoidable, because the ego is being pulled in two opposing directions by the id and the superego. The ego's solution comes in the form of three forms of compromise, one of which is the development of defence mechanisms such as repression, displacement and projection.

Freud's psychosexual theory of development

Freud also proposed a theory of infantile sexuality. This has five distinct, unconscious stages:

i. The oral stage (0–1 year)

ii. The anal stage (1–3 years)

iii. The phallic stage (3–5/6 years)

iv. The latency stage (5/6 years to puberty)

v. The genital stage (puberty to maturity).

During the phallic stage, a boy subconsciously experiences the Oedipus complex and a girl the Electra complex.

Alternative psychodynamic theories

Other theories include:

- ego psychology (Anna Freud, 1936);
- psychosocial theory (Erikson, 1950, 1968);
- analytic psychology (Jung, 1964);
- individual psychology (Adler, 1927).

ISSUES TO BE CONSIDERED

▲ Figure 9.2

Strengths of the psychodynamic perspective

✔ This perspective shows the importance of the unconscious mind as an influence on behaviour, and so allows psychologists to suggest why certain individuals behave in ways that they cannot easily explain or understand.

✔ The perspective lends itself to the use of the case study method, which allows for an in-depth, detailed study of an individual or small group (by gathering both quantitative and qualitative data).

✔ The perspective allows psychologists to suggest causes for mental disorders.

✔ The perspective allows psychologists to study and understand how behaviours can develop over time, as a result of unconscious forces.

Weaknesses of the psychodynamic perspective

✗ This perspective is unscientific in its analysis of human behaviour, as many of the central concepts and theories are subjective and impossible to test scientifically.

✗ The perspective's frequent reliance on the case study method means that sample sizes are small, therefore unrepresentative, so findings are specific and rarely generalisable beyond the participants of the study.

✗ The frequent reliance on case studies also means that evidence is often highly subjective, and can be affected by researcher bias, making the validity of findings questionable.

✗ Studies that can be viewed from this perspective often raise ethical issues, particularly in relation to long- and short-term psychological harm.

▲ **Figure 9.3** Studies from the psychodynamic perspective often raise ethical issues regarding psychological harm to participants

Exam-style questions linked to the psychodynamic perspective

Section C

(a)

   (i) Outline the psychodynamic perspective. **[2]**

   (ii) Describe **one** assumption of the psychodynamic perspective. **[2]**

   (iii) Describe **one** implication of the psychodynamic perspective. **[2]**

(b)

   (i) Describe how the psychodynamic perspective could explain multiple personality disorder. **[4]**

   (ii) With reference to Thigpen and Cleckley's study, describe how the psychodynamic perspective could explain multiple personality disorder. **[4]**

   (iii) Describe how the psychodynamic perspective might explain phobias. **[4]**

   (iv) With reference to Freud's study, describe how the psychodynamic perspective might explain phobias. **[4]**

   (v) Describe how the psychodynamic perspective could explain multiple personality disorder as a defence mechanism. **[4]**

   (vi) Describe how the psychodynamic perspective might explain aggression. **[4]**

(c)

   (i) Describe **one** similarity and **one** difference between any studies that can be viewed from the psychodynamic perspective. **[6]**

   (ii) Describe **one** similarity and **one** difference between any core studies that could be viewed from the psychodynamic perspective. **[6]**

   (iii) Describe **one** similarity and **one** difference between the study by Freud and the study by Thigpen and Cleckley. **[6]**

(d)

   (i) Discuss strengths **and** weaknesses of the psychodynamic perspective, using examples from any studies that can be viewed from this perspective. **[12]**

   (ii) Discuss strengths **and** weaknesses of the psychodynamic perspective, using examples from any of the core studies that might be viewed from this perspective. **[12]**

   (iii) Discuss strengths **and** weaknesses of the psychodynamic perspective, using examples from Thigpen and Cleckley's and/or Freud's study. **[12]**

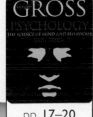

pp. 17–20

▲ **Figure 9.4** How might the psychodynamic perspective explain phobias?

References

BANDURA, A., ROSS, D. and ROSS, S. (1961) Transmission of aggression through imitation of aggressive models. *Journal of Abnormal and Social Psychology*, vol. 63, no. 3, pp. 575–82.

BANYARD, P. and FLANAGAN, C. (2008) *OCR Psychology AS Core Studies and Research Methods*. The Psychology Press.

BARON-COHEN, S., JOLLIFFE, T., MORTIMORE, C. and ROBERTSON, M. (1997) Another advanced test of theory of mind: evidence from very high functioning adults with autism or Asperger Syndrome. *Journal of Child Psychology and Psychiatry*, vol. 38, no. 7, pp. 813–22.

DEMENT, W. and KLEITMAN, N. (1957) The relation of eye movements during sleep to dream activity. An objective method for the study of dreaming. *Journal of Experimental Psychology*, vol. 53, no. 5, pp. 339–46.

FREUD, S. (1909) Analysis of a phobia of a five-year old boy. *Pelican Freud Library*, vol. 8, Case Histories 1.

GRIFFITHS, M.D. (1994) The role of cognitive bias and skill in fruit machine gambling. *British Journal of Psychology*, vol. 85, pp. 351–69.

HILL, G. (2009) *AS and A Level Psychology through Diagrams*. Oxford University Press.

LOFTUS, E. and PALMER, J. (1974) Reconstruction of automobile destruction. *Journal of Verbal Learning and Verbal Behaviour*, vol. 13, pp. 585–9.

MAGUIRE, E.A., GADIAN, D.G., JOHNSRUDE, I.S. and GOOD, C.D. (2000) Navigation-related structural changes in the hippocampi of taxi drivers. *Proceedings of the National Academy of Science, USA*, vol. 97, no. 8, pp. 4398–403.

MILGRAM, S. (1963) Behavioural study of obedience. *Journal of Abnormal and Social Psychology*, vol. 67, no. 4, pp. 371–8.

OCR Specification for GCE Psychology H168 & H568. Version 4. www.ocr.org.uk

PILIAVIN, I., RODIN, J. and PILIAVIN, J. (1969) Good Samaritanism: an underground phenomenon? *Journal of Personality and Social Psychology*, vol. 13, no. 4, pp. 289–99.

REICHER, S. and HASLAM, S.A. (2006) Rethinking the psychology of tyranny. The BBC prison study. *British Journal of Social Psychology*, vol. 45, pp. 1–40.

ROSENHAN, D. (1973) On being sane in insane places. *Science*, vol. 179, pp. 250–8.

SAMUEL, J. and BRYANT, P. (1984) Asking only one question in the conservation experiment. *Journal of Child Psychology and Psychiatry*, vol. 25, no. 2, pp. 315–318.

SAVAGE-RUMBAUGH, S., McDONALD, K., SEVCIK, R.A., HOPKINS, W.D. and RUPERT, E. (1986) Spontaneous symbol acquisition and communication in Pygmy Chimpanzees (Pan paniscus). *Journal of Experimental Psychology*, vol. 115, no. 3, pp. 211–35.

SPERRY, R. (1968) Hemisphere deconnection and unity in conscious awareness. *American Psychologist*, vol. 23, pp. 723–33.

THIGPEN, C. and CLECKLEY, H. (1954) A case of multiple personality. *Journal of Abnormal and Social Psychology*, vol. 47, pp. 135–51.

Note to teachers and students: The references here only cover the Core Studies and other revision guides and textbooks. For a complete list of references please refer to Richard Gross's *Psychology: The Science of Mind and Behaviour*.